The Books

of the

Bible

David Alouidor

ISBN 978-1-0980-9557-4 (paperback)
ISBN 978-1-0980-9558-1 (digital)

Christian Faith Publishing, Inc.
832 Park Avenue
Meadville, PA 16335
www.christianfaithpublishing.com

Printed in the United States of America

Introduction

The Bible is the greatest work of literature, history, and theology ever written. In its production, preservation, proclamation, it stands as the most unique book in existence. It is unity out of a diversity of authors. In the Bible, there are testaments: the Old and the New Testament.

It's a great pleasure for us to introduce the Old Testament, from the first book of Genesis to Malachi, and the New Testament, from Matthew to Revelation, including the details—introduction, author, date and setting, theme and purpose, key word, key verses, and many more. In a very short time, you will be able to study all the sixty-six books in the Bible, from Genesis to Revelation.

Genesis

Genesis is the book of the beginnings. Its fifty chapters sketch human history from creation to Babel (chs. 1–11) and from Abraham to Joseph (chs. 12–50). The first eleven chapters introduce the Creator GOD and the beginnings of life, sin, judgment, family, worship, and salvation. The remainder of the book focuses on the lives of four patriarchs of the faith: Abraham, Isaac, Jacob, and Joseph, from whom will come the nation of Israel and, ultimately, the Savior Jesus Christ.

Introduction and title

The first part of Genesis focuses on the beginning and spread of sin in the world and culminates in the devastating flood in the days of Noah. The second part of the book focuses on God's dealings with one man, Abraham, through whom God promises to bring salvation and blessing to the world. Abraham and his descendants learn firsthand it is always safe to trust God in times of famine and feasting, blessing and bondage. From Abraham...to Isaac...to Jacob...to Joseph... God's promises begin to come to fruition in a great nation possessing a great land. *Genesis* is a Greek word meaning "origin, source, generation, or beginning." The original Hebrew title *Bereshith* means "in the beginning."

Author

Although Genesis does not directly name its author, Genesis ends three centuries before Moses was born. The whole Scripture and church history are unified in their adherence to the Mosaic authorship of the book.

The Old Testament is replete with both direct and indirect testimonies to the Mosaic authorship of all five books of the Pentateuch (Exod. 17:14, Lev. 1:1–2, Num. 33:2, Deut. 1:1, Josh. 1:7, 1 Kings 2:3, 2 Kings 14:6, Ezra 6:18, Neh. 13:1, Dan. 9:11–13, Mal. 4:4). The New Testament also contains many testimonies (Matt 8:4; Mark 12:26; Luke 16:29; John 7:19; Acts 26:22; Rom. 10:19; 1 Cor. 9:9, 23:15). The early church openly held the Mosaic authorship as does the first-century Jewish historian Josephus. As would be expected, the Jerusalem Talmud supports Moses as author.

It would be difficult to find a man in all range of Israel's life who was better prepared or qualified to write this history. Trained in the "wisdom of the Egyptians" (Acts 7:22), Moses had been providentially prepared to understand and integrate, under the inspiration of God, all the available records, manuscripts, and oral narratives.

Date and setting

Genesis is divided into three geographical settings: (1) the Fertile Crescent (chs. 1–11); (2) Israel (chs. 12–36); and (3) Egypt (chs. 37–50).

The setting of the first eleven chapters changes rapidly as it spans more than two thousand years and fifteen hundred miles and paints the majestic acts of the creation, the garden of Eden, the Noahic flood, and the towering citadel of Babel.

The middle section of Genesis rapidly funnels down from the broad brim of the two millennia spent in the Fertile Crescent to less than two hundred years in the little country of Canaan. Surrounded by the rampant immorality and idolatry of the Canaanites, the godliness of Abraham rapidly degenerates into gross immorality in some of his descendants.

In the last fourteen chapters, God dramatically save the small Israelite nation from extinction by transferring the "seventy souls" to Egypt so they may grow and multiply. Egypt is an unexpected womb for the growth of God's chosen nation.

Genesis spans more time than any other book in the Bible; in fact, it covers more than all sixty-five other books of the Bible put together.

Utilizing the same division noted above, the following dates can be assigned.

A. 2000 or more years, 4000–2090 BC (chs. 1–11)
B. 193 years, 2090–1897 BC (chs. 12–36)
C. 93 years, 1897–1804 BC (chs. 37–50)

Theme and purpose

The theme of Genesis is God's choice of a nation through which the whole world would be blessed.

Over two thousand years are covered in Genesis chapters 1–11, but this represents only one-fifth of the book. By contrast, four-fifths of Genesis (chs. 12–50) covers less than three hundred years. It is clear that Genesis is highly thematic, concentrating on the course of God's redemptive work. Genesis is not a complete or universal history.

Genesis was written to present the beginning of everything except God: the universe (1:1); man (1:27); the Sabbath (2:2–3); marriage (@:22–24); sin (3:1–7); sacrifice and salvation (3:15, 21); the family (4:1–15); civilization (4:16–21); government (9:1–6); nations (11); Israel (12:1–3). It was written also to record God's choice of Israel and his covenant plan for the nation so Israel would have a spiritual perspective. Genesis shows how the sin of man is met by the intervention and redemption of God.

Keys to Genesis

Key word—*beginnings*. Key verses—Genesis 3:15, 12.

> And I will put enmity between you and the woman, and between your seed and her seed; he shall bruise your head, and you shall bruise his heel. (3:15)

> I will bless those bless you, and I will curse him who curses you; and in you all the families of the earth shall be blessed.(12:3)

Key chapter—15. Central to all of Scripture is the Abrahamic covenant, which is given in chapter 12 verses 1–3 and ratified in chapter 15 verses 1–21. Israel receives three specific promises: (1) the promise of a great land, from the River of Egypt to the great river Euphrates (15:18); (2) the promise of a great nation, "and I will make your descendants as the dust of the earth" (13:16); and (3) the promise of a great blessing, "I will bless you and make your name great; and you shall be a blessing" (12:2).

Christ in Genesis

Genesis moves from the general to the specific in its messianic predictions: Christ is the seed of the woman (3:15), from the line of Seth (4:25), the son of Shem (9:27), the descendant of Abraham (12:3), of Isaac (21:12), of Jacob (25:23), and of the tribe of Judah (49:10).

Christ is also seen in people and events that serve as types. (A type is a historical fact that illustrates a spiritual truth.) "Adam is a type of him who was to come" (Rom. 5:14). Both entered the world through a special act of God as sinless men. Adam is the head of the old creation; Christ is the head of the new creation. Abel's acceptable offering of a blood sacrifice points to Christ, and there is a parallel in his murder by Cain. Melchizedek ("righteous king") is made like the son of God (Heb. 7:3–7). He is the king of Salem who brings bread and wine and the priest of the Most High God. Joseph also is a type of Christ. Joseph and Christ are both special objects of special love by their fathers, both are hated by their brothers, both are rejected as rulers over their brothers, both are conspired against and sold for silver, both are condemned though innocent, and both are raised from humiliation to glory by the power of God.

Contribution to the Bible

Genesis provides a historical perspective for the rest of the Bible by covering more than all the other biblical books combined. Its sweeping scope from Eden to Ur to Haran to Canaan to Egypt makes it the introduction, not only of the Pentateuch but to the Scriptures as a whole. Genesis gives the foundation for all the great doctrines of the Bible. It shows how God overcomes man's failure under different conditions. Genesis is especially crucial to an understanding of Revelation because the first and last three chapters of the Bible are so intimately related.

Survey of Genesis

Genesis is not so much a history of man as it is the first chapter in the history of redemption of man. Genesis is a highly selective spiritual interpretation of history. Genesis is divided into four great events (chs. 1–11) and four great people (chs. 12–50).

The four great events

Chapters 1–11 lay the foundation on which the whole Bible is built and center on four key events:

I)   *Creation.* God is sovereign Creator of everything, energy, space, and time. Man is the pinnacle of the creation.

II) *Fall.* Creation is followed by corruption. In the first sin, man is separated from God (Adam from God), and in the second sin, man is separated from man (Cain from Abel). In spite of the devastating curse of the fall, God promises hope for redemption through the seed of the woman (3:15).

III) *Flood.* As man multiplies, sin also multiplies, until God is compelled to destroy humanity with the exception of Noah and his family.

IV) *Nations.* Genesis teaches the unity of the human race. We are all children of Adam through Noah, but because of the rebellion at the Tower of Babel, God confuses their culture and language and scatters people over the face of the earth.

Four great people

Once the nations are scattered, God focuses on one man and his descendants through whom he will bless all nations (chs. 12–50).

I) *Abraham.* The calling of Abraham (12) is the pivotal point of the book. The three covenant promises God makes to Abraham (land, descendants, and blessing) are foundational to his program of bringing salvation upon the earth.

II) *Isaac.* God establishes his covenant with Isaac as the spiritual link with Abraham.

III) *Jacob.* God transforms this man from selfishness to servanthood and changes his name to Israel, the father of the twelve tribes.

IV) *Joseph.* Jacob's favorite son suffers at the hands of his brothers and becomes a slave in Egypt. After his dramatic rise to the rulership of Egypt, Joseph delivers his family from famine and brings them out of Canaan to Goshen.

Genesis ends on a note of impending bondage with the death of Joseph. There is a great need for the redemption that is to follow in the book of Exodus.

Outline

I. Creation of heaven and earth (1:1–2)
   A. Creator and creation (1:1–2)
   B. Six days of creation (1:3–31)
   C. Seventh day, day of consecration (2:1–3)
II. The human family in and outside of the garden (2:4–4:26)
   A. The man and woman in the garden (2:4–25)
   B. The man and woman expelled from the garden (3:1–24)
   C. Adam and Eve's family outside the garden (4:1–26)
III. Adam's family line (5:1–6:8)
   A. Introduction—creation and blessing (5:1–2)
   B. "Image of God" from Adam to Noah (5:32)
   C. Conclusion—procreation and perversion (6:1–8)
IV. Noah and his family (6:9–9:29)
   A. Righteous Noah and the corrupt world (6:9–12)
   B. Coming judgment but the ark of promise (6:13–7:10)
   C. Worldwide flood judgment (7:11–24)
   D. God's remembrance and rescue of Noah (8:1–14)
   E. Exiting the ark (8:15–19)
   F. Worship and the word of promise (8:20–22)
   G. God's covenant with the new world (9:1–17)
   H. Noah's sons and future blessing (9:18–29)
V. The nation and the tower of Babylon (10:1–11:26)
   A. Table of nations (10:1–32)
   B. Tower of Babylon (11:1–9)
   C. Family line of Abram (11:10–26)
VI. Father Abraham (11:27–25:11)
   A. Abram's beginnings (11:27–32)
   B. The promissory call of and Abram's obedience (12:1–9)
   C. Abram and Sarai in Egypt, blessing begins (12:10–13:1)
   D. Abram and Lot part—promises recalled (13:2–18)
   E. Abram rescues Lot—Abram's faithfulness (14:1–24)
   F. Covenant promises confirmed (15:1–21)
   G. Abram's firstborn son, Ishmael (16:1–16)

Exodus

—— ⌈⌉ ——

Introduction

The title "Exodus" is an Anglicized version of the Greek word that means "departure" in recognition of one the book's major events—the departure of God's people from Egypt. Exodus could be considered the central book in the Old Testament because it records God's act of saving the Israelites and establishing them as a covenant community, a nation chosen to serve and represent him. Exodus describes the enslavement and oppression of the Israelites; the preparation and call of Moses; the conflict between Yahweh, the God of Israel, and the gods of Egypt (represented by Pharaoh); the exodus of the Israelites; their establishment as a nation in covenant with the Lord; their rebellion; and the Lord's provision for their ongoing relationship symbolized by his presence at the tabernacle that they built for him.

Circumstances of writing

Author

The book of Exodus does not mention who the author was. It does refer to occasions when Moses made a written record of events that took place and what God had said (17:14; 24:4, 7; 34:27–28). The book also contains references to preserving and passing on information. Along with the other four books of the Pentateuch, it has long been considered to be primarily the work of Moses. Moses could have written Exodus at any time during the forty-year time, after the Israelites finished constructing and dedicating the tabernacle at Mount Sinai, at the start of their second year after leaving Egypt (1445 BC) and before his death in the land of Moab (about 1406 BC).

Background

Exodus picks up where the Genesis narrative ended with the death of Joseph around 1805 BC. It quickly moves us forward almost three hundred years to a time when the circumstances of Jacob's descendants had changed in Egypt. The Israelites were serving as slaves during Egypt's Eighteenth Dynasty, probably under the pharaohs Thutmose and Amenhotep II. The Hebrew slaves experienced a miraculous deliverance by God's hand through his servant leader Moses. The Israelites' slavery ended in 1446 BC. The book of Exodus records the events surrounding the Exodus from Egypt and the Israelites' first year in the wilderness, including the giving of the law.

The date of the Exodus is disputed, but biblical evidence favors 1446 BC. First Kings 6:1 states that the exodus occurred 480 years before Solomon's fourth year as king, established by biblical data combined with Assyrian chronology to be 966 BC. In Judges 11:26, Jephthah said that Israel had been living in the region of Palestine for three years. Jephthah lived around 1100 BC, thus dating the end of the wilderness journey around 1400 BC.

Message and purpose

The book of Exodus shows God at work with the goal of having such close relationship with people that he is described as dwelling among them. He rescued the Israelites in order to make himself known, not only by the exercise of his power but also through an ongoing covenant relationship based on his capacity for patience, grace, and forgiveness. The record of what the Lord did for the Israelites provided ground for them to recognize him as their God who deserved their complete loyalty and obedience. This record would make clear to the Israelites their identity as God's people and continue to glorify him.

Exodus conveys four strong messages:

I.   *The Lord God.* God revealed himself to Moses and Israel as Yahweh, "I Am Who I Am." This covenant name for God carries profound meaning and affirms the power, authority, and eternal nature of God.

II. *Redemption.* The Israelites prayed for deliverance, and God responded. God worked through his servant-leader Moses, but he did it in such a miraculous way that it was obvious that God was at work. The Israelites could not save themselves; it was all God's work. The Passover was established to serve as an annual reminder of God's work on their behalf.

III. *Law.* The law of God is encapsulated in the Ten Commandments, God's absolutes for spiritual and moral living. The law is divided into two sections: the civil law, rules that govern life in the community, and the ceremonial law, the patterns for worship and building the tabernacle.

IV. *Tabernacle.* God gave specific instructions how the tabernacle was to be built, but its significance is in what it represented—God dwelling among his people. It was specifically understood to dwell in the Holy of Holies, inaccessible to the normal Israelite. The tabernacle points ahead to the moment when Christ removed the veil of separation, giving all believers access to God. In the New Testament, believers become the tabernacle, for God doesn't dwell among people; He dwells in them.

Contribution to the Bible

Exodus provides the high point of redemptive history in the OT. Many patterns and concepts from Exodus receive attention, further development, and fulfillment elsewhere in Scripture, especially in the past, present, and future work of the Lord Jesus. These include rescue from oppression, provision of sustenance, God's faithfulness to his promise, the self-revelation of God resulting from his actions, the presence of God, his glory, efforts required to preserve God's knowledge, a new identity for people that is based on God's actions, provision for worship, provision for life in community, connection between the reputation of God and his relation with a group of people, obedience and rebellion, intercession, and gracious forgiveness.

Structure

Exodus is considered a part of the law, but it is more historical narrative than the law. The book is structured around the life and travel of Moses. Sandwiched between the narratives of chapters 1–18 and 32–40 are the establishment of the covenant (chs. 19–24) and the laws related to the tabernacle and priesthood.

Outline

I. Oppression of God's people in Egypt (1:11–11:10)
   A. Egyptian slavery (1:1–22)
   B. Preparation of the deliverer (2:1–4:31)
   C. Struggles with the oppressor (5:1–11:10)
II. Deliverance of God's people from Egypt (12:1–14:31)
   A. Redemption by blood (12:1–51)
   B. Redemption by divine miracles (13:1–14:31)
III. Education of God's people in the wilderness (15:1–18:27)
   A. Israel's song of victory (15:1–21)
   B. Testing and trials (15:22–17:16)
   C. Shared leadership under Moses (18:1–27)
IV. Consecration of God's people at Sinai (19:1–34:35)
   A. Acceptance of the law (19:1–31:18)
   B. Breaking of the law (32:1–35)
   C. Restoration of the law (33:1–34:35)
V. Worship of God's people in the tabernacle (35:1–40:38)
   A. Gifts and workmen for the tabernacle (35:1–40:38)

B. Construction and finishings of the tabernacle (36:1–39:43)
C. Filling of the tabernacle with God's glory (40:1–38)

Leviticus

Introduction

The book's name from the Septuagint (the Greek translation of the Old Testament) means "relating to the Levites." This third section of the Pentateuch deals primarily with the duties of the priests and the service of the tabernacle, but it contains other laws as well. Leviticus gives us regulations for worship, laws on ceremonial cleanness, moral laws, and holy days.

Circumstances of writing

Author

Although the book of Leviticus is technically anonymous, the evidence from the Bible and Jewish and Christian traditions attributes it to the law-giver, Moses (ch. 18:5 with Rom. 10:5). Moses was the chief recipient of God's revelations in the book of Leviticus (1:1, 4:1). Elsewhere, Moses is said to have written down revelation that he received (Exod. 24:4, 34:28; Mark 10:4–5, 12:19; John 1:45, 5:46). The author of Leviticus was someone well acquainted with the events in this book, and he was knowledgeable of the Sinai wilderness, making him most likely firsthand witness.

Background

About one year passed from the time Israel arrived at Sinai until they departed (Exod. 19:1, Num. 10:11). During that time, Moses received the covenant from the Lord, erected the tabernacle (Exod. 40:17), and received all the instructions in Leviticus and in the early chapters of Numbers. This block of material is the continuous narrative extending from Exodus 19 through Leviticus to Numbers 10:11. Since these events occurred in just one year, and yet received the largest amount of space in the book from Exodus through Deuteronomy, Moses showed the special importance of the Sinai revelation to the writing of the Pentateuch. The repeated expression "The Lord spake to Moses" throughout Leviticus leaves no doubt that its instructions were divine in origin, not the creation of Moses (Lev. 1:1, 27:1).

Message and purpose

The message and purpose of Leviticus must be studied in the context of the redemption of Israel from Egypt (Exod. 12), the covenant made with Israel (Exod. 20–24), and the building of the tent of meeting or tabernacle (Exod. 25–40). The Lord dwelt among Israel symbolically in the tent of meeting, which stood in the center of the camp's tribal arrangement. In order for the Lord to reside with Israel, it was imperative that the people maintain a holy character and ethical behavior (Lev. 11:44–45, 19:2; Deut. 23:14; 1 Pet. 1:15–16). The decrees in Leviticus instructed the people in regulating this holy relationship through atonement and ritual cleansing. The sacrifices, the ordination of the holy priests, the purity of the laws, and the code for holy living made benevolence of the Lord a reality through forgiveness of sin and ceremonial purification. The purpose of Leviticus was to instruct Israel to holiness so that the Lord might abide among them and bless them. Five key words capture the message of Leviticus:

I. *Holiness.* The chief idea in Leviticus is the holiness of God. The priests were to teach the people to differentiate "between the holy and the common, and the clean and the unclean" (10:10). "Holy" describes special persons (priests), places (tent), or things (offerings) that are captivated by or share in God's presence. Thus the holiness of everything and everyone is contingent upon the Holy One who alone is inherently holy. Anything that compromises this exclusive relationship profanes (treats as common) the person or thing and offends God, who is apart and who sets apart (makes holy [22:16]).

II. *Clean.* "Clean and unclean" are ritual terms that pertain to physical substances. Any item that was a departure from its normal state was unclean. This included certain foods, skin diseases, bodily emissions, and contamination. Consequently, rites of purgation ("cleansing") were a feature of daily life and constant reminders of the inadequacy of the people to maintain their relationship with God apart from his provision.

III. *Sacrifice.* The sacrifices were holy gifts presented to the Lord. They also made atonement and provided stipends for the priests and communal meals. The three voluntary offerings were the burnt, grain, and fellowship sacrifices; the required offerings were the sin and restitution offerings. Special additional instructions for sacrifices applied to special events.

IV. *Atonement.* The term "to atone," or "make atonement," means "to reconcile two estranged parties." Theologically, God is the aggrieved party and must be appeased by the offender (26:14–45). The Lord provided the means by which the affront could be remedied and forgiven (4:20; 19:22). Genuine remorse and confession of sin were required (5:5, 16:21, 26:40–42), not just ritual performance (Hos 6:6, Mic. 6:8, Matt 9:13).

V. *Priests.* The Levites were the priests' assistants in caring for the tabernacle (Num. 8:13, 19, 22). It was the priest who made atonement on the guilty person's behalf (Lev. 4:20) as well as for himself (16:6, 24). Their role of protecting the holiness of God, the sanctity of the tent and the Israelite people, is illustrated by the intercessory action of Aaron who "stood between the dead and living" (Num. 16:48).

Contribution to the Bible

Leviticus is often neglected because Christians have misunderstood its message and purpose. This was not true of Jesus, who designated "love your neighbor as yourself" (19:18) as the second greatest commandment (Matt 22:39). The Apostle Paul considered these words the summation of the Mosaic Commandments (Rom. 13:9, Gal 5:14, James 2:8). The writer of Hebrews relied on images of Leviticus in describing the person and role of Jesus Christ: sacrifice, the priesthood and the day of atonement (Heb. 4:14–10:18). Studying Leviticus gives us a deeper devotion to Jesus Christ, a stronger worship of God, and better understanding of daily Christian living.

Structure

Leviticus is primarily a collection of laws with a little historical narrative. The laws contained in Leviticus can be divided into two groups. First is commands, or apodictic law. These are both positive commands ("you must…") and negative commands ("you must not…"). The second type of law is casuistic law. These are case laws using an example of what to do if such and such happened ("if a man…"). Some scholars seek to divide the laws further into civil laws, moral laws, and ceremonial laws, but there is no evidence that the Israelites made such a distinction

Outline

   I.   Laws on sacrifices and the priesthood (1:1–7:38)
      A.   Introduction on different offerings (1:1–6:7)
      B.   Regulations for the priests (6:8–7:38)
  II.   Ordination and ministry of the priests (8:1–10:20)
      A.   Consecration of Aaron (8:1–36)
      B.   Dedication of the tabernacle (9:1–24)
      C.   Warning about immoral priests (10:1–20)

III. Laws on purity (11:1–16:34)
  A. Clean and unclean animals (11:1–47)
  B. Purification for uncleanness (12:1–15:33)
  C. Regulation for the Day of Atonement (16:1–34)
IV. God's requirements for holiness (17:1–27:34)
  A. Reverence for blood (17:1–16)
  B. Obedience to the Lord's commands (18:1–22:33)
  C. Appropriate worship (23:1–26:46)
  D. Making and keeping vows (27:1–34)

Numbers

Introduction

The English title "Numbers" derived from the Septuagint name *Arthmoi*, based on the two military censuses in chapter 1 and 26. The Hebrew title *Bemidbar*, "in the wilderness," describes the geographical setting of much of the book—from the wilderness of Sinai to the plains of Moab, across the Jordan River from Jericho.

Circumstances of writing

Author

Christians scholars have traditionally held that Moses was the author of the Pentateuch, which includes the book of Numbers. As with the other books in the Pentateuch, Numbers is anonymous, but Moses is the central character throughout. Moses kept a journal (33:2), and the phrase "The Lord spoke to Moses" is used thirty-one times. It is possible that a few portions were later added by scribes, such as the reference to Moses's humility (12:3) and the reference to the "book of the Lord's wars" (21:14). Moses remained the primary writer.

Background

Numbers continues the historical narrative begun in Exodus. It picks up one month after the close of Exodus (Exod. 40:2, Num. 1:1), which is about one year after the Israelites' departure from Egypt.

Numbers covers the remaining thirty-nine years of the Israelites' stay in the wilderness, from Sinai to Kadesh and, finally, to the plains on the eastern side of the Jordan river.

Message and purpose

Sovereignty of God. The principal character in the book of Numbers is Yahweh, the God of Israel. He is sovereign over the affairs of all peoples from all nations. Even Balaam, a sorcerer opposed to the ways of God, was made into an instrument for accomplishing his purposes. God will accomplish his will even when his people rebelled, as in the rejection of the promised land in chapters 13–14. In the end, he kept his promise to Abraham by achieving this goal in the next generation of Israelites.

Presence Of God. God's presence is exemplified in the pillar of fire by night and the pillar of cloud by day, by the ark of the covenant that represents the throne of his presence among humanity, and by the mobile sanctuary which demonstrates that the God of Israel cannot be confined to a territory, region, or city, much less a sanctuary of any kind.

Purity and holiness of God. God is holy and pure, and he requires such behavior from those who claim him as their God. This is a central theme of the Pentateuch and the book of Numbers.

God and revelation. The revelatory terminology of "the Lord spoke to Moses" provides the framework for the structure of the book. Moses is the primary human agent of revelation. Numbers presents God as one who is able to accomplish his revelatory will even through a donkey or a reluctant pagan diviner.

Promise and fulfillment. God said to Abram that He would produce a great nation through him (Gen. 12:2) and give his descendants the land of the Canaanites and Amorites (15:1, 8–21; 17:8). The two censuses show God's fulfillment of the first promise. The granting of territory to two and one-half tribes in the Transjordan is the beginning of the land fulfillment. God proved himself faithful to that second promise by bringing it to fruition for the second generation (Num. 15:1–21, 27:1–23, 36:1–12).

Uniqueness and exclusivity of God. The God of Israel is the one true God, and therefore, He is worthy of humanity's exclusive devotion. He cannot tolerate the worship of other deities, the elements, and forces of creation. He is beyond human reason to comprehend and incomparable to human character (23:19). All images of deities were forbidden by Israelite law, along with unauthorized worship centers, cultist instruments, and certain worship styles. All such forms of idolatry were to be removed from the land, lest Israel lapse into such transgression and suffer punishment.

Celebration in worship. The dual themes of celebration and worship are delineated from the initial chapters of Numbers, which depict Israel in harmonious devotion to Yahweh (chs. 1–7) to the promise of an abundance of crops in the land which would be brought to Yahweh in sacrifices and offerings when the people inherited their tribal territories (15:1–21, 28:1–29:40). Interspersed throughout the book are several songs, including the "song of the cloud" (9:17–23) and the "battle the song of the Ark" (10:35–36). The parameters of faithful worship for the sojourning Israelites are also delineated through several negative circumstances, including failure to keep the Passover (9:13), the breaking of the Sabbath (15:32–41), and the judgment against unfaithful priests or their supporters (chs. 16–17). Worship and celebration of the God of Israel are not limited to Israelites. Several passages state that there is one law for the Israelites and foreigners. They could celebrate the Passover if they wanted to identify with Israel in devotion to Yahweh, the one true God, but they had to abide by his instruction and precepts (9:14).

Contribution to the Bible

Numbers shows us how God responded to the unbelief of the Israelites. There are consequences to our disobedience, but God's grace remains, and his redemptive plan and desire for us will not be stopped. The book of Numbers underscores for us the importance of obedience in the life of a Christian, and Paul reminded us of the value of learning from the way God had worked in the past (Rom. 15:4; 1 Cor. 10:6, 11).

Structure

Numbers reflects the challenging message of faithfulness. The book consists of seven cycles of material, with the repetition of the following types of material: (1) a statement of historical setting, (2) reference to the twelve tribes of Israel and their respective leaders, (3) matters related to the priests and Levites, and (4) laws for defining the nature of the faithful community.

The book of the law is primarily narrative with portions of case law interwoven into vibrant literature fabric.

Outline

I.   First census and consecration of Israel at Sinai (1:1–6:27)
   A.   Numbering and arrangement of the people (1:1–2:34)
   B.   Choosing of the Levites (3:1–4:49)
   C.   Cleansing and blessing of the people (5:1–6:27)

II.   Preparation for departure to the promised land (7:1–10:36)
   A.   Gifts of tribal leaders (7:1–89)
   B.   Consecration of the Levites (8:1–26)
   C.   Observance of the Passover (9:14)
   D.   Movement of the Camp (9:15–10:36)

III.   From Mount Sinai to Kadesh (11:1–15:41)
   A.   Disobedience of the people (11:1–14:45)
   B.   Miscellaneous instructions and laws (15:1–41)

IV.   Rebellion against Aaron's priesthood (16:1–19:22)
   A.   Judgment of Korah, Dathan, and Abiram (16:1–17:13)
   B.   Duties and revenues of priests and Levites (18:32)
   C.   Ordinance of the red cow (19:1–22)

V.   From Kadesh to the plains of Moab (20:1–25:18)
   A.   Rebellion for Moses and Aaron (20:1–29)
   B.   Judgment and healing by snakes (21:1–35)
   C.   Balaam's efforts to curse Israel (22:1–24:25)
   D.   Campaign of Phinehas against idolatry (25:1–18)

VI. Second census and preparation of the new generation (26:1–30:16)
VII. Another counting of Israel (26:1–65)
    A. Inheritance for Zelophehad's daughters (27:1–23)
    B. Instructions to the new generation (28:1–30:16)
VIII. Preparation for entering the promised land (31:1–36:13)
    A. Vengeance against the Midianites (31:1–54)
    B. Settlement of tribes beyond the Jordan (32:1–42)
    C. Journey from Egypt summarized (33:1–49)
    D. Instructions for division of Canaan (33:50–34:29)
    E. Levitical cities and havens of refuge (35:1–34)
    F. Laws of females' inheritance amended (36:1–13)

Deuteronomy

Introduction

The title of this book of the Pentateuch, Deuteronomy, comes from the Septuagint (the Greek translation of the Old Testament) and means "second law." The phrase is actually a mistranslation of 17:18, which reads "a copy of this instruction." It is still a fitting title since all of the book contains repetition of the laws found in Exodus, Leviticus, and Numbers.

Circumstance of writing

Author

The book itself asserts that Moses is the principal source and author for the material (1:1), as do subsequent OT texts (Josh. 1:7–8, 1 Kings 2:3, Ezra 3:2) and NT texts (Matt 9:7, Acts 3:22, Rom. 10:19). This attribution remained unchallenged until the advent of modern rationalism in the seventh and eighteenth centuries, but no argument advanced by this school of thought had successfully overcome the ancient Mosaic tradition.

Background

The Exodus probably occurred in 1446 BC, whereupon Israel set out for Canaan, the inheritance God had promised his people. Because of their rebellious spirit, the Israelites were forced to wander in the desert for forty years (2:7) until at last they arrived in Moab, just opposite Jericho (32:49). It was there Moses put pen to parchment to compose this farewell treatise (31:9, 24).

Message and purpose

Though the initial covenant between the Lord and Israel was made at Sinai, the generation that received it had largely died out in the thirty-eight years since the event. Now the younger generation needed to affirm their commitment to the covenant (4:1–8). Moreover, the transition from a largely nomadic existence in the desert to sedentary lifestyle in Canaan required a covenant revision and expansion suitable to these new conditions. The purpose of Deuteronomy is to provide guidelines to the new covenant community to enable them to live obediently before God and to carry out his intentions for them. Several themes appear through Deuteronomy.

Nature and character of God. The chief attribute of God is holiness. With the Shema (6:4), Israel's confession of faith, the holiness and uniqueness of God is emphasized. There is no God but Yahweh. His holiness and righteousness are reflected throughout the moral nature of his law.

Because he is the only God, he is also completely sovereign. God's sovereignty is especially stressed in light of the covenant relationship. Yahweh is Israel's Sovereign Lord, and he will not share his sovereignty with another, whether person or false god.

Another key attribute of God is his love. His love for his people in seen repeatedly as Deuteronomy recounts the miraculous acts of God on behalf of his chosen people, and his loving acts were designed to bring his people in line with his purpose for them. Closely akin to God's love is his graciousness. God did not have to choose Israel. Even when they complained or were disobedient, God exhibited grace though they did not deserve it.

Covenant relationship. God had entered into relationship with Israel out of love (7:8). In that covenant, as God's people, the Israelites were to reflect their relationship with God by reflecting his character to nations around them. God's election of them as the gift of the land were parts of God's side of the covenant, and obedience and the service were the Israelites' part of the covenant. Deuteronomy gives strong words regarding the blessings of living in the covenant.

Faith response of God's people. The Israelites' response to the covenant relationship with God was to live, both individually and as a nation, in total commitment to the Lord God. There is no area of life that is not under God's sovereign rule. No distinction is made between the religious and the secular, and God expects the highest standard of ethical conduct from the people.

How God's people reflected this would be expressed in obedience to the law. All of the law must be summed up in one command: "Love the Lord with all your heart, with all your soul, and with all your strength" (6:5). God's people should not respond with fearful obedience but with loving obedience. "If you love me, you will keep my commands" (John 14:15). The command to love is grounded in God's love that He demonstrated to them; therefore, loving obedience is natural faith responding to a loving God. We love because he first loved us (1 John 4:19).

Sin and consequences. In Deuteronomy, sin is presented in the context of the covenant. If you fail to follow God's commands, it would disrupt the covenant relationship, affecting its purity, unity, and witness. Disobedience would lead to cursing. Deuteronomy 27–28 gives strong words about what would happen if the people would fail to keep their part of the covenant. The nation as a whole would suffer for their disobedience and apostasy. Their history shows that God carried through with the consequences about which he warned Israel.

Contribution to the Bible

Next to the books of Psalms and Isaiah, the NT allude to Deuteronomy more than any other book in the OT. This is true not only in terms of the sheer number of instances but especially in the passages where theological truth seems mostly the issue. Jesus and the apostles considered Deuteronomy of paramount importance to their own teaching about God and his dealing with the chosen people and humanity at large. Jesus, in his temptation, quotes the book of Deuteronomy three times against Satan (Matt 4:4–10).

Structure

The style of the book of Deuteronomy is a series of repetitious, reminiscent, and even irregular exhortations, which is fitting for a collection of Moses's sermons preparing the people for their move to the promised land. The style is also reflective of the typical suzerain-vassal treaties which could contain a preamble, historical prologue, main provision, blessing and curse, and plan for continuing the covenant relationship. The book of Deuteronomy could be considered the constitution for the nation of Israel once it was established in the promised land.

Outline

I.   First address of Moses (1: 1–4:49)
    A.   Preface and historical introduction (1:1–5)
    B.   Review of Israel's history (1:6–4:49)
II. Second address of Moses (5:1–26:19)
    A.   Series of exhortations (5:1–11:32)
    B.   Series of laws and statutes (12:1–21:23)
    C.   Series of laws for Israel's social life (22:1–26:19)
III. Third address of Moses (27:1–30:20)
    A.   Provision for future renewal of the covenant (27:1–26)
    B.   Covenant blessings and curses (28:1–29:15)
    C.   Final exhortations to obedience (29:16–30:20)
IV. Final days of Moses (31:1–34:12)
    A.   Designation of Moses's successor (31:1–30)
    B.   Song of Moses (32:1–52)
    C.   Moses's final blessings of Israel (33:1–29)
    D.   Death and burial of Moses (34:1–12)

Joshua

— ✑ —

Introduction

The book of Joshua is named for the most famous member of the
Israelites in the generation after Moses's death. The book describes
the history of the generation of Israelites who crossed the Jordan
River and entered the promised land of Canaan. Their battles and
faithfulness have a place among the greatest histories of faith in the
Old Testament. Joshua led the people to defeat the adversaries who
opposed God's people. He then oversaw the division of the land into
the tribal allotments. Finally, Joshua renewed the covenant between
the people and God.

Circumstances of writing

Author

The author of the book of Joshua is not identified in the Bible
and otherwise remains anonymous. If Joshua himself did not originally compose the book that bears his name, then it may be presumed someone who knew him and his exploits recorded the work.
There are many references throughout Joshua that suggest a final
formation of the book after his lifetime. These include Joshua's death
and descriptions of memorials and names that are said to remain "to
this day" (4:9, 5:9, 6:25, 7:26, 8:28–29, 10:27, 13:13, 14:14, 15:63,
16:10, 22:17, 23:8).

Background

The account in the book of Joshua occurred in the period immediately after Moses's death. This was a new generation, not the one that had left Egypt. The Joshua story was set when the nation of Israel first appeared in the land west of the Jordan river—the land that would bear their name. First Kings 6:1 states that the Exodus occurred 480 years before Solomon's fourth year as king (966 BC). In Judges 11:26, Jephthah said that Israel been living in the regions of Palestine for three hundred years. Jephthah lived around 1100 BC, thus dating the end of the wilderness journey and the beginning of the conquest around 1400 BC.

Message and purpose

Commission of a new leader. Chapter 1 establishes Joshua as divinely appointed leader and as Moses's successor. God addressed Joshua directly, promising both the land that he promised Moses (Deut. 34:4) and his divine presence (Josh. 1:3–5). The command to be strong and courageous (1:6, 7, 9) define Joshua's mission. The miraculous crossing of the Jordan River was God's means of exalting Joshua in the eyes of all Israel (4:14).

Holy war. Joshua's military leadership recurs throughout the first twelve chapters of the book. Its theological dimensions raise questions about the extermination of all people from the land. How could a loving God allow such slaughter? Appeals to the sovereignty of God and his wrathful judgment may be made. A complimentary explanation focuses on the exceptions of Rahab's family and of the Gibeonites who escape divine wrath through their confession of faith in Israel's God (2:8; 9:9–10, 24).

Land as an inheritance. Joshua's allocation of the land in chapters 13–21 continued the process already begun by Moses in Transjordan. So far, as God was giving this land to his people as an inheritance, the tribal allotments take on a covenantal character. This land inheritance formed the material wealth of the family of Israel.

The covenant between God and Israel. The covenant making over which Joshua presided dominates the book. It is explicitly detailed in 8:30–35 and 24:1–28. In both of these sections, Joshua's leadership established Israel in a close relationship with God. God's grace enabled the nation to occupy its land and to worship God alone. The circumcision and Passover celebration in chapter 5, as well as the theological role of the tribal allotments as part of Israel's covenantal inheritance from God, suggest that fulfillment of the covenant is an integral part of the book.

God as holy and as deliverer. God's character is evident throughout the book, especially in terms of his holiness and his saving acts. Divine holiness occurs in the ceremonies where God separated Israel from the other nations (4:19–24; 5:1–3, 13–15; 22:26–27; 24:26–27). God's saving acts are clearly presented in the military victories of the people.

Contribution to the Bible

Just as Joshua's leadership begins with Moses's death, so the book of Joshua follows and completes the book of Deuteronomy. Deuteronomy serves as a means by which the new generation of Israelites renewed their covenant with God. The book of Joshua provides the means by which God fulfilled his part of the covenant. God gave them victories, but each victory requires a step of faith. God's provision for the people as their leader and guide bore witness to later generations of the divinely willed leadership for Israel, and his gracious gift of the land showed how the people's faithful fulfillment of the covenant could result in abundant blessing.

Structure

The book Joshua should be seen as a land grant, similar to the land grants and suzerain treaties of the ancient Near East. The suzerain, who was Israel's God, gave to his people the land they were meant to receive. There are three major parts to the structure of the land grant.

First is a review of the histories and events leading up to the gift of the land. This occurs in chapter 1 and its discussion of what has brought Joshua to this point—Moses's death. Chapters 2–5 detailed the preparation for the acquisition of the gift of the land. Chapters 6–12 describe the battles that were fought as background to the receipt of the land. The second section considers the allotment of the territories to the tribes and families of Israel. The many specific names and towns of this part of the text provide a particularity to the gift that affirms it was an authentic fulfillment of God's promise to his people. The third section is a renewal of the covenant. Here, the key parts are the stipulations of the covenant that require loyalty to God alone (24:14–15) and the response of the people that they agree to these demands.

Outline

I. Preparation for the land (1:1–5:12)
    A. Joshua assumes leadership (1:1–18)
    B. Rahab's faith (2:1–24)
    C. Across the Jordan River (3:1–4:24)
    D. Circumcision and Passover (5:1–12)

II. Victory in the land (5:13–12:24)
    A. Success against Jericho (5:13–6:27)
    B. Failure of Achan (7:1–26)
    C. Success against Ai (8:1–29)
    D. Covenant renewal (8:30–35)
    E. Failure of Israel and Gibeon (9:1–27)
    F. Victories in the land (10:1–12:24)

III. Allotment of the land (13:1–21:45)
    A. Remaining lands (13:1–27)
    B. Transjordan allotment (13:8–14:5)
    C. Judah's allotment (14:6–15:63)
    D. Joseph allotment (16:1–17:18)
    E. Mapping the remaining land (18:1–10)
    F. Tribal allotment (18:11–19:51)
    G. Cities of refuge (20:1–9)

H. Cities of the Levites (21:1–42)
I. God's promise fulfilled (21:43–45)
IV. Worship of God (22:1–24:33)
    A. Transjordan and the altar of controversy (22:1–34)
    B. Joshua's farewell address (23:1–16)
    C. Israel's covenant at Shechem (24:1–28)
    D. Joshua and his generation die (24:29–33)

Judges

Introduction

The book of Judges is the second of the Historical books in the Old Testament. In the Hebrew Bible, these books are called the former Prophets; the theological and spiritual concerns found in the Pentateuch and the Prophets take precedence over simply recording historical facts. They derived its name from the Hebrew designation of the principal characters, *shiphetim* (2:18), which could also be translated as "governors." These judges were the Lord's agents of deliverance. The Lord is both the central character and the hero of the judges.

Circumstances of writing

Author

No author is named in the book of judges, nor is there any indication given of the writer or writers who are responsible for it. The three divisions of the book are on different footing regarding the sources from which they are drawn. The historical introduction presents a form of the traditional narrative of the conquest of Palestine that is parallel to the book of Joshua. The main portion of the book, comprising the narratives of the judges, appears to be based on oral or written traditions of a local observer.

Background

The period of the Israelite judges lay between the conquest of the promised land under Joshua and the rise of the monarchy with Saul and David. The events described are thus to be dated from the end of the fifteenth century BC to the later part of the eleventh century BC, a period of around three hundred years. This was a time of social and religious anarchy, characterized by the repeated refrain "in those days there was no king in Israel; everyone does whatever he wanted" (17:6, 18:1, 19:1, 21:25).

We cannot say exactly when the book of Judges was written. The reference in 18:30 to the fate of Dan at the time of the exile from the land suggests a date of final editing after the exile of the northern kingdom by Assyria around 722 BC. Meanwhile, the suggestion that readers could visit the site of Gideon's altar at Ophrah in 6:24 suggests a date prior to the exile of the southern kingdom, Judah, in 586 BC. Its message would have resonated strongly at several points of Israel's history, and it has been argued that it fits well during the dark days of Manasseh (686–642 BC [2 Kings 21:1–18]). However, it not possible to date Judges with precision.

Message and purpose

The book of Judges chronicles the moral and spiritual descent of Israel from the relative high point at the beginning of the book through a series of downward spirals to the depths of degradation in chapters 17–21. Though God raised up a sequence of deliverers, the judges, they were unable to reverse this trend, and some even became part of the problem themselves. By the end of the book, Israel had become as pagan and defiled as the Canaanites they had displaced. If this trend continued, it would only be a matter of time before the land would vomit them out, as it had the Canaanites before them (Lev. 18:28).

Human depravity. The book of Judges demonstrates what happens to the Lord's people when everyone does whatever they want. It shows that Israel cannot presume upon God's grace, and neither can we. If we abandon his commandments and pursue the idols of our own imagination, the result will be moral and spiritual chaos. This is where we would all end if the Lord left us to ourselves.

The grace of God. The book of Judges offers profound commentary on God's grace. Left on their own devices, the Israelites would surely have destroyed themselves. Only by repeated gracious intervention of God did they emerge from the dark premonarchic period as a people and nation distinguishable in lifestyle and belief from surrounding pagan groups.

The need for God's leadership. While it is possible that the repeated refrain "there is no king in Israel" (17:6, 18:1, 19:1, 21:25) paints this book as an appeal for a monarchy, it is better to see it as a call to return to God as King. Rather than lifting up the kings as an ideal above the confusion of this period, the addition of "everyone did whatever he wanted" (17:6, 21:25) reduced the population to the moral and spiritual level of Israel's kings in later years. In other words, rebellion against God is democratized. Israel did not need a king to lead them into sin; they could fall into immorality on their own. The Israelites abandoned the God of the covenant to follow the fertility gods of the land. The writer, by exposing this problem, sought to wake up his own generation. This is an appeal to the covenant people to abandon all forms of paganism and return to Yahweh.

Contribution to the Bible

The book of Judges shows us that the nation of Israel survived the dark days of the judges entirely by God's grace. In mercy, he sent oppressors as reminders of their rebellion. In mercy, he responded to their cries and raised up deliverers. Judges also illustrates the fundamental problem of the human heart. When God's people forget his saving acts, they go after other gods. Judges also illustrates the link between spiritual commitments and ethical conduct. In the end, the book of Judges illustrates the eternal truth: the Lord will build his kingdom in spite of our sin and rebellion.

Structure

The book falls into three parts. There is a prologue (1:1–3:6) that deals with the failure of the second generation to press on with the conquest of Canaan. This is followed by a sixfold cycle of sin and salvation (3:7–16:31), which forms the bulk of the book. Finally, there is an appendix (chs. 17–21) that shows the full effects of total depravity let loose upon the people. This structure demonstrates not only the repetition of patterns of sin and judgment but also negative progress. The midpoint of the narrative is the linked episode involving Gideon and Abimelech which serves to highlight further the significance of the issue of kingship.

Outline

    I.   Prologue (1:1–3:6)
        A.   Israel's failure to possess the land (1:1–36)
        B.   The pattern of sin, judgment, and restoration (2:1–3:6)
   II.   The judges (3:7–16:31)
        A.   Othniel (3:7–11)
        B.   Ehud (3:12–30)
        C.   Shangar (3:31)
        D.   Deborah and Barak (4:1–5:31)
        E.   Gideon and Abimelech (6:1–9:57)
        F.   Tola and Jair (10:1–5)
        G.   Jephthah (10:6–12:7)
        H.   Ibzan, Elon, and Abdon (12:8–15)
        I.   Samson (13:1–16:31)
  III.   Epilogue (17:1–21:25)
        A.   The religious degeneration of Israel (17:1–18:31)
        B.   The moral degeneration of Israel (19:1–21:25)

Ruth

Introduction

The book of Ruth gets its name from one of its principal characters, a Moabite woman named Ruth who was the ancestor of David and Jesus. After reading the book of Judges, which paints a dark and depressing picture of Israel, the reader is relieved to encounter Ruth. Although the book is relatively short, it is rich in examples of kindness, faith, and patience. It is one of the five scrolls that was to be read during the Jewish festivals, in particular, the Festival of Weeks.

Circumstances of writing

Author

The Talmud attributes the authorship of Ruth to Samuel, but the book itself offers no hint of the identity of its author. We can only speculate about who might have written the book of Ruth, and its provenance and date must be deduced from the internal evidence—language and style, historical allusion, and themes. The genealogy at the end and the explanation of archaic customs require a date during or later than the reign of King David (1011–971 BC), though it could have been written as late as after the exile when the issue of the inclusion of the Gentiles once again became pressing.

Background

The book of Ruth is set "during the time of the judges" (1:1), a period of social and religious disorder "when everyone did whatever he wanted" (Judg. 17:6). Historically, this era bridged the time between the conquest of the land under Joshua and the rise of King David, whose genealogy forms the conclusion of the book. It is not clear exactly when during the time of the judges the book belongs, but it opens with a famine in the land, which may have been the result of Israel's idolatry.

Message and purpose

Grace. Naomi thought that the Lord's hand of judgment was upon her after she and her husband left the promised land in search of food and married their sons to Moabite women in search of offspring (1:21). She underestimated God's grace. Her daughter-in-law, Ruth the Moabitess, turned out to be the means by which the Lord would meet her needs for food and offspring to carry on the family name. Ruth's choice of a place to glean, which seemed to be a matter of chance, turned out to be a divine appointment with Boaz, the man who would fulfill the role of family redeemer for Naomi and Ruth.

The book of Ruth resembles the parable of the lost son (Luke 15:11–32) in two strands. The family of Elimelech wandered away from the land where the Lord had promised to bless his people in search of fullness. As a result, however, Naomi ended up empty and alone. Yet the Lord's judgment on her was designed to bring her back home and to replace her emptiness with a new fullness. Similarly, the book of Ruth opens with the Lord's people experiencing the trials of the days of the judges when general disobedience led to famine. Yet the Lord graciously provided food for his hungry people and a king to meet their needs for leadership. These are lessons that speak to us as well.

We too have gone astray from the Lord and need to receive his grace and mercy.

God's providence. The genealogy of David at the end of the book shows that the Lord worked through this story to provide for his people's need of a king. Even though the Lord's actions are mainly concealed, there are two specific events attributed to him—providing food for his people (1:6) and conception for Ruth (4:13). In these ways, the Lord provided for all his people's needs.

Faithful love. The book of Ruth demonstrates how the Lord shows his covenant faithfulness to his undeserving people, often in surprising ways. In the course of the narrative, each of the main characters proved to be a person of extraordinary courage and covenant love; *faithful, lovingkindness, loyalty* are the key words of this book (1:8, 2:20, 3:10). These are people whose spiritual commitment is demonstrated clearly in godly living.

Family redeemer. The book of Ruth provides a great example of a family member who used his power under Jewish law to redeem. Boaz demonstrated one of the duties of the family member—that is, marrying the widow of a deceased family member. A correlation is sometimes made between the redemption of Ruth by Boaz and the redemption of sinners by Christ. Because of God's covenant faithfulness, he has provided the redeemer that we all need in Jesus Christ. Jesus is the true King toward whom the genealogy of David will ultimately extend (Matt 1:5–6), and he is the redeemer in whom his wandering people find rest. In him, the Gentiles too are incorporated into the people of God by faith and granted a place in the family of promise.

Contribution to the Bible

Ruth's covenantal faithfulness to Naomi and her God provided a model showing that those who were not ethnic Israelites could be incorporated into God's people through faith. If Moabites who joined themselves to the Lord could be accepted, then other Gentiles are as well (Isa. 56:3–7). The book also effectively answered questions that may have been raised over the legitimacy of the Davidic line given his Moabite roots.

Structure

The book is a delightful short story with a classical plot that moves from crisis to complication to resolution. The narrator draws the reader into the minds of the characters (successively, Naomi, Ruth, Boaz), inviting us to identify with their personal anxieties and joy and, in the end, to celebrate the movement from emptiness and frustration to fulfillment and joy.

Outline

  I.   Scene 1—Moab (1:1–22)
       A.   Elimelech's departure (1:1–5)
       B.   Naomi's despair (1:6–13)
       C.   Ruth's decision (1:14–22)
  II. Scene 2—fields of Bethlehem (2:1–23)
       A.   Ruth meets Boaz (2:1–14)
       B.   Boaz provides for Ruth and Naomi (2:15–23)
  III. Scene 3—Boaz's threshing floor (3:1–18)
       A.   Boaz's desire to marry Ruth (3:1–11)
       B.   Marriage delayed (3:12–18)
  IV. Scene 4—City of Bethlehem (4:1–22)
       A.   Boaz marries Ruth (4:1–12)
       B.   Ruth gives birth to Obed (4:13–15)
       C.   Naomi is blessed with a new family (4:16)
       D.   Ruth is an ancestor of David (4:17–22)

1 Samuel

Introduction

The books 1 and 2 Samuel highlight a significant transition time in Israel's history. As 1 Samuel begins, Israel is a loosely organized tribal league living under poor spiritual leadership. God's plan for his people nonetheless continues as he raised up Samuel to guide Israel's transition from theocracy to a monarchy. Saul's kingship constitutes the remainder of First Samuel, while David's kingship is largely the focus of Second Samuel.

Circumstances of writing

Author

Early tradition suggests 1 and 2 Samuel were originally one book. Some scholars believed Samuel was largely responsible for the material up to 1 Samuel 25, and that the prophets Nathan and Gad gave significant input to the rest (based on 1 Chron. 29:29). This proposal, however, must remain speculative because the books don't name any authors. First Samuel 27:6 suggests the book was not completed until perhaps a few generations after the division of the kingdom around 930 BC.

Background

After Israel's conquest of the land during the days of Joshua, Israel entered a time of apostasy. The book of Judges describes recurrences of a cycle with predicable phases. First, the people sinned against the Lord and fell in idolatry. Second, the Lord raised up an adversary to afflict them and return them to him. Third, the people cried out to the Lord in repentance. Fourth, the Lord brought deliverance for them through a judge whom he raised up. The book of Judges' famous verse, "in those days there was no king in Israel; everyone did whatever he wanted" (Judg. 21:25), aptly describes the period. First Samuel picks up the historical record toward the end of those stormy days.

Message and purpose

Leadership. The books of 1 and 2 Samuel provide numerous examples of good and bad leadership. When leaders focused their attention on the Lord and saw their leadership roles as instruments for his glory, they flourished; when they abandoned the Lord and used their offices for their own gain, they failed. The lives of Eli and his sons, plus the lives of Samuel, Saul, David, and others consistently illustrate these principles.

God's sovereignty. The books of 1 and 2 Samuel highlight God's provision at Israel's every turn. He provided good spiritual leadership through Samuel, and he provided Israel its first king, though kingship was not his perfect will for his people at that time. He provided his people the leaders and resources they needed to defeat their enemies and to live out his purpose in the land, though both people and leaders often failed him.

Sin's consequences. The books of 1 and 2 Samuel take sins seriously, describing in detail the awful consequences of sin—even forgiven sin. Saul's disobedience of God led to his estrangement from his son Jonathan and from David and ultimately led to his death in battle. David's sin with Bathsheba, though forgiven, brought consequences that haunted David the rest of his life.

Covenant. The books of 1 and 2 Samuel describe God's relationship with his covenant people and his faithful response to the terms of that covenant. The Lord also established a special covenant with David, a covenant that ultimately would find its fulfillment in the Lord Jesus Christ.

Contribution to the Bible

The books of 1 and 2 Samuel describe Israel's transition from a loosely organized tribal league under God (a theocracy) to centralized leadership to a king who answered to God (a monarchy). Samuel's life and ministry greatly shaped this period of restructuring as he consistently pointed people back to God.

Saul's rule highlighted the dangers to which the Israelites fell victim as they clamored for a king to lead them. Samuel's warnings fell on deaf ears (1 Sam. 8:10–20) because God's people were intent on becoming like other nations around them. In the end, they got exactly what they asked for, but they paid a terrible price. Saul's life stands as a warning to trust God's timing for life's provisions.

David's rule testified to the amazing works the Lord could and would do through a life yielded to him. Israel's second king seemed quite aware of God's blessing on his life and displayed a tender heart toward God's things (2 Sam. 5:12, 7:1–2, 22:1–51, 23:1–7). Later generations would receive blessing because of David's life (Isa. 37:35). God's special covenant with David (2 Sam. 7:1–29) found ultimate fulfillment in Jesus, the son of David (Luke 1:32–33). The consequences of David's sin with Bathsheba, however, stand as a warning to all who experience sin's attraction. God holds his children accountable for their actions, and even forgiven sin can have terrible consequences.

Structure

The first seven chapters of 1 Samuel describe Samuel's birth, call, and initial ministry among the Israelites. Chapter 8 is a major turning point as the people ask for a king to rule them, the same as the other nations (1 Sam. 8:5). Chapters 9–12 describe Saul's selection—at God's direction, yet not his perfect will for the time (1 Sam. 12:16–18).

First Samuel 13–31 describes Saul's victories and failures. Saul was a king with great physical stature and military skill (1 Sam. 14:47–52), but his heart was not one with the Lord (1 Sam 13:14). His unwillingness to obey the Lord's commands ultimately outweighed his accomplishments, and chapters 16–31 describes his reign's downward spiral. During this time, God raised up David and was preparing him for the day he would succeed Saul—a fact Saul gradually realized (1 Sam. 15:28, 24:20–21, 28:17).

Second Samuel 1–4 describes the struggle for Israel's throne that began with Saul's death. David was anointed king by the men of Judah (2 Sam. 2:4), but Abner anointed Ish-bosheth, Saul's oldest surviving son, as king over Israel (2 Sam. 2:8–9). A two-year civil war resulted in Ish-bosheth's death and in David becoming king all over Israel.

Second Samuel 5–24 presents highlights of David's reign. God established a special covenant with David, promising to establish the throne of his kingdom forever (2 Sam. 7:1–29). David's sin with Bathsheba, however, brought disastrous consequences to his reign and became a turning point in 2 Samuel. In the end, David's repentance confirmed his designation as a man after God's heart, but his sin showed even the king is not above the law.

Outline of 1 Samuel

I. Samuel's ministry (1:1–12:25)
   A. Samuel's birth and call (1:1–#:21)
   B. The ark narrative (4:1–7:17)
   C. The people ask for a king (8:1–12:25)
II. Saul's reign (13:1–31:13)
   A. Saul's battles with the Philistines (13:1–14:52)
   B. Saul's failure against the Amalekites (15:1–35)
   C. David's selection as Saul's successor (16:1–23)
   D. David's victory over Goliath (17:1–58)
   E. David's struggles with Saul (18:1–26:25)
   F. Saul's reign end (27:1–31:13)

2 Samuel

See introduction to 1 Samuel for the introductory material.

Outline of 2 Samuel

I.   David's activities after Saul's death (1:1–4:12)
  A. David grieves for Saul and Jonathan (1:1–27)
  B. David in Hebron as king of Judah (2:1–4:12)
II. David as king of Judah and Israel (5:1–15:6)
  A. David's military successes (5:1–10:19)
  B. David's great sin and its consequences (11:1–13:39)
  C. David's problems with his son Absalom (14:1–15:6)
III. Absalom's rebellion and David's final days as king (15:7–24:25)
  A. Insurrection and Absalom's death (15:7–19:8)
  B. David returns to Jerusalem as king (19:9–20:26)
  C. Events of David's latter days (21:1–24:25)

1 Kings

Introduction

The titles of these books are certainly descriptive of their contents: the history of the kings and the kingdom of Judah. Originally, these two books were just one book but were divided by the translators of the Septuagint (the Greek translation of the Old Testament). The First and Second Kings are parts of a larger body of the Old Testament known as twelve Historical books (Joshua–Esther).

Circumstances of writing

Author

The scholars cannot identify the authors of any portions of these books. Traditional guesses such as Samuel and Jeremiah lack evidence, although a prominent worshiper of Yahweh like Jeremiah would have been influential in the circles that produced these books. Since the books clearly incorporated many earlier documents, the complete authorship would be all writers who contributed to the source documents of this work. At some points, the Holy Spirit worked in the human authors to authenticate the inspired, inerrant books of 1 and 2 Kings. The final stage of composition or compilation had to come after the release of Jehoiachin from Babylonian imprisonment (ca. 562 BC). That edition may have added only a postscript to a work completed years earlier, or it may have involved significant additions.

Background

The history recorded in 1 and 2 Kings covers approximately 410 years. First Kings begins around 970 BC with the death of King David, and 2 Kings ends around 560 BC with the release of King Jehoiachin from prison. During this time, the nation of Israel split into two kingdoms (930 BC), and both kingdoms went into exile (Israel in 722 BC and Judah in 587 BC).

Message and purpose

The theological perspective of 1 and 2 Kings is expressed in a number of themes: (1) the sinfulness of the king and nation, (2) the conflict between the demands of practical politics and the demands of faith, (3) the glory that God gave to the obedient covenant kings, (4) God's harshness in judgment on some occasion and leniency on others, and (5) the conflict between the worship of the Lord and worship of the gods.

The role of the kings. The Davidic covenant established the king as the moral representative of the people for covenant purpose. Therefore, up through kings Azariah (also known as Uzziah) and Jotham, the moral state of the king was treated as equaling the moral state of the people. Covenant blessings were given or withheld on the basis of the king's behavior. Thus the behavior of the king was the important covenant and moral fact for a given reign.

The role of the prophet. This was a period of development of the office of the prophet. The nature of the prophetic office passed through several nonconsequential stages, from the ecstatic, miracle-working prophets represented by Saul (1 Sam. 19:24) and Elisha (2 Kings 3:14–16), then through miracle-working court prophets such as Gad and Micaiah and, finally, to the great writing prophets attested in Scripture.

Revival. The last two revival kings of Judah (Hezekiah and Josiah) experienced individual revivals that had few effects on either the rest of the royal house or on the nation as a whole. The nation returned to apostasy on the death of each of these good kings. Therefore, these two revivals did not bring full restoration of international political power and wealth. Rather, they simply delayed the inevitable judgment.

Contribution to the Bible

For the Bible writers, history could not have existed without God's purposes. This makes all history theological. The books 1 and 2 Kings interpreted Hebrew history in light of OT covenant theology. The Babylonian exile created the need for this work of historical apologetics. The exiles needed to explain the failure of the religious program established by the sovereign God. In Deuteronomic history—Joshua, Judges, 1 and 2 Samuel, and 1 and 2 Kings—this failure was consistently explained as the failures of the people to live up to their part of the covenant.

Structure

The organizing principle of 1 and 2 Kings is not story or narrative. Kings is unique because its basic structural units were the formulaic royal records. Formal openers (1 Kings 15:9–10) and closers (1 Kings 15:23–24) usually identify the boundaries of these records. Then the writer could insert other types of literature before, between, and after the openers and closers: narrative, prayers, descriptions, etc. But the most important element was the elevation of the ruler's faithfulness to the covenant (1 Kings 15:11–15). All of these materials made up history of covenant obedience or disobedience.

Outline of 1 Kings

    I.   Final days of King David (1:1–2:11)
        A.   Adonijah tries to seize the throne (1:1–38)
        B.   Solomon anointed as David's successor (1:39–53)
        C.   David's charge to Solomon (2:1–11)
   II.   Solomon's reign over the united kingdom (2:12–11:43)
        A.   Solomon deals with his opponents (2:12–46)
        B.   Solomon's wisdom (3:1–28)

C. Solomon's officials (4:1–19)
D. Solomon's splendor (4:20–34)
E. Solomon builds the temple (5:1–8:66)
F. Solomon's fame and reputation (9:1–10:29)
G. Solomon's sin and death (11:1–43)
III. Divided kingdom of Judah and Israel (12:1–22:53)
A. Judah's King Rehoboam (12:1–24)
B. Israel's King Jehoboam (12:25–14:20)
C. King Rehoboam of Judah continued (14:21–31)
D. Judah's Abijam and Asa (15:24)
E. Israel's Nadab and Baasha (15:25–16:7)
F. Israel's Elah, Zimri, Tibni, and Omri (16:8–28)
G. Israel's King Ahab and the Prophet Elijah (16:29–22:40)
H. Judah's King Jehoshaphat (22:41–50)
I. Israel's King Ahaziah (22:51–53)

2 Kings

Introduction

See the introduction to 1 Kings for the introductory material.

Outline of 2 Kings

II. The kingdom of Judah—from King Hezekiah to the cap-
tivity (18:1–25:30)
   A. Revival under Hezekiah and apostasy (18:1–21:26)
   B. Revival under Josiah and apostasy (22:1–25:7)
   C. Jerusalem falls to the Babylonians (25:8–30)

1 Chronicles

Introduction

The word *Chronicles* in Hebrew has the meaning of "an ongoing account," almost like a journal or diary or minutes taken at a meeting. They are the first and second books of a four-book series that includes Ezra and Nehemiah. Together these four books provide a priestly history of Israel from the time of Adam to the rebuilding the house of God and the walls of Jerusalem. At one time, the book of Chronicles was probably one single scroll, which was divided later for convenience by those who translated the Old Testament into Greek (the Septuagint).

Circumstances of writing

Author

An ancient tradition ascribes the authorship of Chronicles to Ezra. The author must have lived sometime after the return of the Jews to Israel from the Babylonian exile. He also had a strong interest in the reimplementation of the law and the temple, and he must have had access to historical records. All of these criteria suit Ezra, and this identification is corroborated by the fact that the last verses of Chronicles note we will refer to him simply as "the chronicler."

Background

The books of 1 and 2 Chronicles include extensive genealogies from the time of Adam and take the reader up to the period of the nation's exile and restoration. First Chronicles gives us the genealogies and focuses on the reign of King David. Second Chronicles focuses on all the kings who followed David up to the exile and restoration. It covers the same time period as 1 and 2 Kings, but Second Chronicles focuses exclusively on the king of Judah. The content of the books necessitates that they were written sometime after the return from exile, perhaps the middle of the fifth century BC.

Message and purpose

Having resettled in Jerusalem after the exile, the people needed to reconnect with their identity as God's people. Chronicles met this purpose by reminding them of their heritage and directing them back to God's presence in their midst as symbolized by the temple. The important ideas that 1 and 2 Chronicles emphasize are: (1) a direct connection to God's people in the past, (2) the continuity of the line of David on the throne of Judah, (3) the centrality of the temple and its rituals in focusing on God, (4) the importance of music in worshiping God, (5) the invincibility of God's people when they obey him, and 6) the inevitability of punishment when God's people disobey him.

The books 1 and 2 Chronicles convey several key themes. These include

- *God's control of history.* God desires to dwell among his people in a perfect relationship of holiness in which he is God and redeemer of his people. The tabernacle and the temple symbolize that desire, a desire that was ultimately fulfilled through Jesus Christ—the son of David. Chronicles shows how God worked from the time of Adam but particularly in the time of David through Ezra and Nehemiah to accomplish his desire to dwell in holiness with his people.

- *Covenant with David.* God chose David and his lineage to build his house. The final ruler in this lineage is the son of David—the Messiah. Solomon built the temple in Jerusalem, but it is Jesus who is building and shall build the completion of God's true house. Christ is the one who will reign forever. His people are those of Israel and indeed of all nations who will put their trust in him.

- *The holy God is to be worshipped properly.* The two books of Chronicles show us that the God who dwells in holiness must be approached according to the law that God gave to Moses. David, in seeking to unite his people around God's presence, learned that God must be sought in the proper way. Worship by way of the altar of sacrifice as ministered by the Levitical priesthood was important, and the place of the altar of sacrifice was to be in Jerusalem at the threshing floor of Ornan (Araunah). There David erected the altar, and Solomon built the temple according to God's directions.

- *The house of God.* The books of Chronicles intended to encourage God's people to work together with God and with one another to build God's house. The people were challenged through these books to go up to Jerusalem to build God's house. Chronicles remind the people of God's history of faithfulness to his people and to his house. God promised that he would bless their obedience to this challenge.

Contribution to the Bible

Chronicles brings together many dimensions of biblical revelation, such as historical events (as recounted in Genesis through Kings), temple ritual (as prescribed in Leviticus), sin and judgment (as preached by the prophets), and even some psalms. Because a recurring theme is that God will always accept people who return to him no matter how wicked they may have been, it has been called, perhaps a little whimsically, the Gospel according to Ezra. The books of 1 and 2 Chronicles give us the big picture of OT history, capturing the Davidic covenant in light of Israel's history back to Adam, and pointing to the eternal continuation of that covenant through the reign of the Messiah.

Structure

The Hebrew Bible divides its books into three categories: the Law, the Prophets, and the Writings. In this arrangement, the books of Samuel and Kings are counted among the Prophets, whereas Chronicles belong to the Writings. This classification may be partially due to the fact that Chronicles repeats information, such as genealogies of Genesis and the histories of the kings of Judah from the books of Samuel and Kings. Still the Chronicler uses the repeated content to support his own point, and he also adds a lot of information that we find in Chronicles alone. He limits his discussion of the various kings entirely to those of Judah, the southern kingdom.

Outline of 1 Chronicles

I.   The genealogies (1:1–9:44)
    A.   Genealogies of the human race (1:1–54)
    B.   Genealogies of the twelve tribes (2:1–9:44)
II. Reign of David (10:1–29:30)
    A.   Fall of Saul's house and rise of David (10:1–14:17)
    B.   Removal of the ark to Jerusalem (15:1–16:43)
    C.   David's desire to build God's house (17:1–27)
    D.   David's victories over Israel's enemies (18:1–21:30)
    E.   David's preparations for building the temple (22:1–19)
    F.   Arrangement for the service of the Levites (23:1–26:32)
    G.   David's final days (27:1–29:30)

2 Chronicles

Introduction

See the introduction to 1 Chronicles for the introductory material.

Outline of 2 Chronicles

I. Reign of Solomon (1:1–9:31)
   A. Solomon builds the temple (1:1–7:22)
   B. The glory of Solomon's kingdom (8:1–9:31)
II. The reign of Solomon's successors (10:1–36:23)
   A. Rehoboam (10:1–12:16)
   B. Abijah (13:1–22)
   C. Asa (14:1–16:14)
   D. Jehoshaphat (17:1–20:37)
   E. Jehoram (21:1–20)
   F. Ahaziah and Athaliah (22:1–12)
   G. Joash (23:1–24:27)
   H. Amaziah (25:1–28)
   I. Uzziah (26:1–23)
   J. Jotham (27:1–9)
   K. Ahaz (28:1–27)
   L. Hezekiah (29:1–32:33)
   M. Manasseh (33:1–20)
   N. Amon (33:21–25)
   O. Josiah (34:1–35:27)
   P. Last kings of Judah (36:1–23)

Ezra

Introduction

The books of Ezra and Nehemiah bear the names of the key person in each of the books. Until the third century AD though, the books Ezra and Nehemiah were regarded as a single book. Both books contain material found in the other, and they complete each other. The separation of the book in the Christian community took place through the influence of the Vulgate, the Latin translation prepared by Jerome who, following Origen before him, separated Ezra-Nehemiah into two distinct books. In the Jewish community, Ezra and Nehemiah were not separated into two distinct books until the fifteenth century printing of the Hebrew Bible. In the Hebrew Bible, Ezra-Nehemiah is part of the third division of the canon, called the Writings (Hebrew, *Ketuvim*).

Circumstances of writing

Author

The Ezra and Nehemiah authors are anonymous. Ancient Jewish sources usually credit Ezra as the author of Ezra-Nehemiah. More likely, Ezra-Nehemiah was written by the Chronicler, the person (or persons) responsible for 1 and 2 Chronicles. Not only is Ezra-Nehemiah linked to Chronicles at its introduction (Ezra 1:1–2, 2 Chron. 36:22–23), it also shared many similarities in language, terminology, themes, and perspective.

Background

It is probably safe to assume that Ezra-Nehemiah was written soon after the conclusion of Nehemiah's ministry. Most likely, the book was written no later than 400 BC.

In Ezra-Nehemiah, it is clear that Ezra came to Jerusalem first, probably in 458 BC, and that Nehemiah followed him thirteen years later, probably 445 BC. Nehemiah made no mention of Ezra, his ministry, or his reforms. Ezra and Nehemiah appear together in only two texts (Neh. 8:9, 12:36). The two events Ezra and Nehemiah were together were significant. In Nehemiah 8, the context is reading of the laws to the people, while in Nehemiah 12, the two joyous processions walking around the city walls in the dedication ceremony include Ezra (Neh. 12:36) and Nehemiah (Neh. 12:38).

Message and purpose

Ezra continues where 2 Chronicles left off. While it provides us with key historical insights, it is rich in message for God's people.

The continuity of God's people. The events in Ezra-Nehemiah connect the Israelites with the preexilic community. The returning exiles experienced a new exodus and remained a part of God's redemptive plan. God even used pagan leaders like Cyrus and Artaxerxes to restore his people.

Holiness. For the people to continue the covenant relationship with God, it was important for them to separate and remain pure in matters of doctrine, ethic, and customs. Prior to the exile, the people experienced judgment because of their ability to remain faithful single-mindedly in their relationship to their covenant God. Ezra-Nehemiah shows us a renewed interest in remaining separated unto God.

Scripture. Ezra and Nehemiah reaffirm the centrality of the law and practice of the Israelite community. They knew the authority of the Scripture, but they were called back from their neglect of its teachings. Multiple times they showed that the people worked and behaved in accordance with what Moses had written (Ezra 3:2, 6:18;

Neh. 8:14–15, 13:1–3). Ezra and Nehemiah may give us the best example of the power of God at work through the written word.

Worship. The returning exiles built an altar to sacrifice to God before they rebuilt the temple. Only after the place was finished did they rebuild the walls. They got the projects in proper order because worship and proper relationship with God precede everything else.

Prayer. Alongside worship is an abundance of prayer in these books. Two extensive prayers are recorded (Ezra 9, Neh. 9). Prayer and fasting are mentioned multiple times as they set out on their task, and the whole rebuilding of the wall was bathed in prayer. Prayer is combined with action throughout Nehemiah, and both books underscore the need to approach God constantly in prayer.

Contribution to the Bible

The events which occurred in Ezra and Nehemiah—the rebuilding of the temple, the stabilizing of Jerusalem, and the Jewish community that developed—all played key roles in ministry's life and Jesus's ministry recorded in the Gospel. The rebuilding of the temple may have paled in comparison to Solomon's temple, but it would serve the Jews for centuries until Christ removed the need for a physical temple.

Structure

Ezra-Nehemiah was written in related but distinct languages—Hebrew and Aramaic. The Hebrew sections generally reflect the style of the postexilic era with some evidence of the impact of Aramaic on the language. Aramaic, a Semitic language similar to Hebrew, occurs in two sections in the book of Ezra (Ezra 4:8–6:18, 7:12–26). During the Persian period (ca. 540–330 BC), Aramaic was the official language of diplomacy and commerce.

Ezra-Nehemiah is similar to Samuel and Kings, and especially Chronicles, in that many sources were utilized in its composition. These include two major types of sources. Much of Ezra-Nehemiah consist of material from the Ezra and the Nehemiah Memoir. The

Ezra Memoir, usually written in first person, include Ezra 7–10, along with Nehemiah 8, and probably chapter 9 as well, but embedded in this memoir are lists and records from other sources used by Ezra. The composition of the Nehemiah Memoir is regarded as including Nehemiah 1–7 as well as 11–13. But here also Nehemiah incorporated lists and records in his memoir. Ezra-Nehemiah also contains many lists, genealogies, inventories, letters, and census records throughout the book. For a community that attempted to reestablish itself after the disaster of 586 BC and the subsequent exile to Babylon, material was crucial in recording their life as a community.

Outline of Ezra

I. Return from exile (1:1–6:22)
  A. The decree of Cyrus (1:1–11)
  B. Exiles who returned (2:1–70)
  C. Restoration for worship (3:1–13)
  D. Opposition (4:1–24)
  E. Rebuilding the temple (5:1–6:22)
II. Reform through Ezra (7:1–10:44)
  A. Ezra's arrival (7:1–10)
  B. Artaxerxes's letter (7:11–28)
  C. Returnees with Ezra (8:1–14)
  D. Search for Levites (8:15–20)
  E. Preparing to return 8:21–30)
  F. Arrival in Jerusalem (8:31–36)
  G. Sin and confession (9:1–10:44)

Nehemiah

See introduction to Ezra for the introductory material.

Outline of Nehemiah

I.   Rebuilding the walls (1:1–6:19)
    A. Jerusalem's plight and Nehemiah's prayer (1:1–11)
    B. Nehemiah's mission (2:1–10)
    C. Surveying the walls (2:11–20)
    D. Rebuilding begun (3:1–32)
    E. Opposition and oppression (4:1–6:19)

II.   Restoration for the community (7:1–13:31)
    A. Repopulating Jerusalem (7:1–73a)
    B. The covenant renewed (7:73b–10:39)
    C. Repopulating Jerusalem continued (11:1–21)
    D. Essential records (11:22–36)
    E. Temple personnel (12:1–26)
    F. Dedication of the wall (12:27–47)
    G. Nehemiah's further reforms (13:1–31)

Esther

Introduction

Esther is a unique book. It is the only book in the Bible that never mentions God, although his presence is implied due to Mordecai's allusion to divine providence (4:14). At times the book seems rather secular; historically, this has contributed to questions regarding its place in the canon of the synagogue and the church. Esther is tightly connected with specific historical events, yet it is also a piece of literature, a narrative with all of the literary features necessary to make it a great story. It is a book in which its purposes are not always explicitly stated but are derived from the story as a whole.

Circumstances of writing

Author

Like most of the OT books, the author of the book is unknown. In the Jewish Talmud, it is suggested that the members of the great synagogue wrote the book. However, it is hard to imagine this prestigious group of religious scholars writing a book that mentions the Persian king 190 times but never mentions God. Many early writers, both Jewish as well Christian, suggested Mordecai as the author.

Background

Esther's story is rooted in the historical situation of King Xerxes (Ahasuerus), who ruled as king in Persia from 486–465 BC.

Mid-twentieth-century critical scholars tended to date the book late, even into the second century BC. However, most argue for an earlier date. The discovery of the Dead Sea Scrolls in 1947 showed that the Hebrew of Esther was very different from the Hebrew from the first century BC. Also, there are no Greek words in the text of Esther, which would suggest that it was written before Alexander the Great's conquest (ca. 333 BC) made Greek the language of the region. Most likely, the book was written in the fourth century BC.

The book gives every indication of being a historical narrative. For that reason, the alleged historical anomalies in the text raised for many interpreters problems in accepting the historicity of the story. While it is regrettable not to have any extant extra-biblical confirmation of the main characters in the story (Esther, Haman, Mordecai), several points must be considered.

First, there are few extant Persian records for Xerxes's reign. Thus very few historical figures are known from this time. Moreover, the Greek writers, especially Herodotus, were writing their history particularly related to Greeks, not as court historians for the Persians; thus, their material is selective and would leave unmentioned many significant figures. Second, the absence of extra-biblical evidence does not mean these people did not exist. Third, while there is no positive extra-biblical confirmation of these individuals, they appear in an account that even ardent critics acknowledge as being remarkably accurate in its description of the Persian era.

Message and purpose

The principal message of the book of Esther called all Jews to celebrate Purim. Esther's purposes can be distinguished into two types: those purposes that pertain to the original audience of the book during the Persian period and the broader theological purposes that transcend the book's original readers.

Hope. For the Jewish people scattered around the Persian Empire, the book of Esther was a story that gave encouragement and hope. It provided a model of how Jews could not merely survive but also thrive in a Gentile environment. It showed how Jewish people could effectively serve in positions of high responsibility while maintaining their Jewish identity and their commitment to the God of Israel. It showed how Jewish leaders could be used to bring blessing to their Gentile and ruler neighbors. And for a people far from the land of their forefathers, it demonstrated that the God of Israel was still able to redeem his people in their oppression, whether they were in Egypt, Israel, or Persia.

Divine providence. It is unlikely the lack of any mention of God in the book is accidental. It leaves the reader to ponder God's work, evident but unseen, in the unfolding story of deliverance and redemption. This is fitting since Jews in exile would be tempted to find lack of evidence for God's ever presence to be evidence for his actual absence. The book of Esther counters this notion, depicting God's providence as ruling even the events of foreign lands during exile.

God's unlikely instruments. Part of the mystery of God's providence in the book is how God can use such unlikely people to help accomplish his plans. Who would ever guess that a young Jewish woman named Hadassah (Esther), an orphan, would end up as the queen of the greatest empire the world had ever known? Who but God could bring about such a powerful reversal through the "weakness" of a young woman?

Contribution to the Bible

Without ever mentioning God directly, the book of Esther underscores God's providence. God's promises to give the Jews an eternal ruler remained in place, even in the face of threatened annihilation. Esther shows us that many Jews remained faithful to their God even in exile. They kept their identity as God's people through the synagogues that developed as the centers of the Jewish community wherever Jews settled. The synagogues would later play a significant role as the Gospel spread throughout the Roman Empire, for these served as natural starting places for the deliverance of the Gospel in the towns visited by the apostles (e.g., Acts 9:20, 17:1–2, 18:19, 19:8).

Structure

The Hebrew of the Masoretic Text used as the basic Holman Standard Bible is a fairly straightforward text. It is written in a form of late biblical Hebrew common to the postexile era and found in other biblical books of that time, such as Chronicles, Ezra-Nehemiah, and Daniel. Like Ezra-Nehemiah, Esther shows the growing influence of Aramaic in its grammar and vocabulary as well as the presence of many Persian words.

Outline

I.   Replacement queen (1:1–2:20)
    A. Vashti angers the king (1:1–12)
    B. The king's decree (1:13–22)
    C. Search for a new queen (2:1–14)
    D. Esther becomes queen (2:15–20)

II.   A dangerous threat (2:21–3:15)
    A. Mordecai saves the king (2:21–23)
    B. Haman's plan to kill the Jews (3:1–15)

III. Esther's daring decision (4:1–5:14)
    A. Mordecai's appeal to Esther (4:1–17)
    B. Esther approaches the king (5:1–14)

IV.   The great reversal (6:1–10:3)
    A. Mordecai honored by the king (6:1–14)
    B. Haman is executed (7:1–10)
    C. Esther intervenes for the Jews (8:1–17)
    D. Victories of the Jews (9:1–32)
    E. Mordecai remembered (10:1–3)

Job

Introduction

The book of Job is named after the central character and speaker. The narrative deals with a man who lost everything and the subsequent discussions he had about the reason for his suffering. God alone had the final word and, eventually, restored all that Job had lost.

Circumstances of writing

Author

The author of Job is unknown. The author was a learned man whose knowledge embraced the heavens (22:12, 38:32–33) and earth (26:7–8; 28:9–11; 37:11, 16). His knowledge touched on foreign lands (28:16, 19), various products (6:19), and human professions (7:6, 9:26, 18:8–10, 28:1–11). He was familiar with plants (14:7–9) and animals (4:10–11, 38:39, 39:30, 40:15–41:34). He was a wise man, familiar with traditional wisdom (6:5–6; 17:5; 28:12, 28), but above all, a man of spiritual sensitivity (1:1, 5, 8; 2:3; 14:14–15; 6:11–21; 19:23–27; 23:10; 34:26–28; 40:1–5; 42:1–6). He was doubtless an Israelite confirmed by his frequent use of God's covenant name (Yahweh).

Background

Job's story is set in the patriarchal period. In that era, wealth consisted of the possession of cattle and servants. Like other OT patriarchal heads, Job performed priestly duties, including offering sacrifices for his family. Like the patriarchs, Job lived to be one hundred years old. Geographically, the action took place in the Northern Arabian Peninsula, in the land of Uz (1:1), often associated with Edom. Job's three friends also had Edomite or southern associations, as did the young Elihu (see notes at 2:11, 32:2–3).

Although Job is set in the patriarchal period, its date of writing is unknown. Jewish tradition places the authorship of Job in the time of Moses.

Message and purpose

The book of Job demonstrates that a sovereign, righteous God is sufficient and trustworthy for every situation in life, even in the most difficult of circumstances. Along with this truth, Job also carries several messages.

Character. A major portion of the book's discussion revolves around conduct that reflects correct ethical values. Job is introduced as a man of character (1:1), and God testified to his consistently blameless character (1:8; 2). In discussing Job's situation, Eliphaz initially suggested that Job's blameless character could prove to be his benefit (4:7). Bildad, however, was not so sure (8:6, 20). Both men later stated that no one can be totally pure (15:14–15, 25:4–5). Job consistently maintained that his conduct was above reproach (27:5, see ch. 31), and he was willing to take his stand before God to prove it (23:7). As Job saw it, in God's dealings with man, He does not appear always to reward a blameless man and pure life (9:23, 10:14).

Righteousness. Job stated that his righteousness was the central issue in his situation (6:29), yet he wondered how he could convince God of this (9:2, 15, 20; 10:15). All three of Job's friends condemned Job's attitude as self-righteous (32:1). For Elihu, Job's fault was failing to see God's essential righteousness while maintaining his own (32:2; 34:5,17). In this, Elihu anticipated God's own words to Job (40:8).

Justice. Job wanted to receive justice in his situation (19:7, 23:4). He renounced injustice (27:4) and modeled justice in his dealing with others (29:14, 31:13–15) but felt that God had not always dealt justly with him (14:3, 16:10–14, 23:14–16, 34:5–6; 35:2). Job wanted to present his case before God (13:18), but he wondered whether he could get a hearing (9:32). Little is said about justice and injustice in the divine speeches, but the conclusion is evident. God's justice is seen in his administration of the physical universe and animal world as well as human relationships. Only God has the wisdom and power to govern all of this with perfect harmony and justice. Rather than championing his own righteousness, Job should understand God's essential righteousness by which he justly administers the universe (40:7–14). When Job finally came to understand this (42:4–6), he experienced the justice he had sought and found his sufficiency in God.

Contribution to the Bible

The book of Job teaches that suffering comes to everyone, the righteous and unrighteous alike. God does not always keep the righteous from danger or suffering. Ultimately, God controls all of life's situations, including the limited power of Satan. God's comfort and strength are always available to the trusting soul.

Although the book of Job does take note of the problem of suffering, it focuses more on the nature of human conduct before a sovereign and Holy God. In harmony of the rest of Scripture, the book teaches that even a consistent practice of religion is insufficient without a genuine heart relationship with God (Deut. 6:4–6, Ps. 86:11–12, Matt 22:37). The answer of life's problems and goals relies in a proper reverence for him who is perfect in all his being and actions. Man needs not just to confess but to surrender everything to him. By letting him truly be the God in every area of life, a person will find him sufficient.

Structure

The writer was a skilled storyteller, artistically characterizing distinctions between the protagonist (Job), antagonist (Satan), and literary foils (the three friends and Elihu). The characterization demonstrates that God himself is the ultimate Protagonist (or "Hero") of the story. Satan was as much as challenging God as Job's piety. Although Job's "three comforters" applies traditional wisdom to Job's situation, each did it in a different way. Eliphaz, the rationalist, reasoned with Job (15:17–18); Bildad, the apologist, sought to defend God (25:1–6); and Zophar acted much like a prosecutor (11:1–6). The youthful Elihu served as a mediating influence in order to prepare for the divine speeches that follow (33:23–26). The writer constructed a well-developed plot built around dramatic dialogue. The fact that he related the account of Job's test in story form does not mean that Job was not a real person who underwent a real test.

Outline

I. Prologue—the setting of the test (1:1–13)
   A. Job's life before the test (1:1–5)
   B. Satan's first accusation and proposed test (1:6–12)
   C. Job's response to the first test (1:13–22)
   D. Satan's second accusation and proposed test (2:1–6)
   E. Job's response to the second test (2:7–10)
   F. The arrival of Job's comforters (2:11–13)
II. Development—examining Job's condition (3:1–27:23)
   A. Job's lament over his condition (3:1–26)
   B. Dialogues about Job's condition (4:1–27:23)
III. Denouement—explaining Job's condition (28:1–37:24)
   A. Job's speeches about his condition (28:1–31:40)
   B. Elihu's speeches about Job's condition (32:1–37:24)
IV. Resolution—Job's condition and God's greatness (38:1–42:6)
   A. God's first speech—his sovereign power (38:1–40:2)
   B. Job's response—his self-renunciation (40:3–5)

Psalms

Introduction

The word for psalms in Hebrew is *Tehilim*, which means "praise." The English title is derived from the Greek translation (LXX) *psalmoi*, which means "songs of praise." Praise directed to Yahweh, the God of Israel, is certainly the primary emphasis in the Psalms. Some had referred to the psalms of Israel's hymnbook, which is partially true but, overall, is insufficient to account for all that is in the Psalms. More than one-third of the collection is made up of prayers to God. Therefore, it contains both hymns and prayers that were used in the context of Israel's worship.

Circumstances of writing

Author

Since the book is a collection of many different psalms written a long time ago, there is not just one author for this collection. By far, the most common designation in the title is Davidic, which may refer to David as the author of those psalms. David's role as a musician in Saul's court (1 Sam. 16:14–23) as well as his many experiences as a shepherd, a soldier, and a king make him a likely candidate for writing many of these psalms.

The problem is that the mention of names in titles consists of an ambiguous Hebrew construction. It is nothing more than a preposition attached to David's name. The preposition could be translated "written by," "belong to," "for," or "about." This does nothing more than relate the psalms bearing that title to David in some way but not necessarily naming him as the author. The translation "Davidic" accurately conveys this same ambiguity.

Other titles include the designation of Solomon (Pss. 72, 127), Asaph (Pss. 50, 70–83), the songs of Korah (Pss. 42, 44–49), Ethan (Ps. 89), Heman son of Korah (Ps. 88), and Moses (Ps. 90. All of these use the same Hebrew preposition as appears with David's name and, therefore, have the same ambiguity about authorship. In Asaph's case, although he was one of David's chief musicians (1 Chron. 6:39), the name itself became associated with a group of musicians bearing the same name (Ezra 2:40–41); see note at Psalm 50 title. This might explain why an apparently postexile (Ps. 74) includes the title "of Asaph."

Background

The book of Psalms consists of many different hymns and prayers composed by individuals but used by the community. If one were to take the name in the title as author, the date of composition ranges from the time of Moses (fifteenth century BC) to a time following the exile (six century BC or later). Some of the titles do contain historical information that might indicate the setting of the composition, although even this (like the authorship) is ambiguous. They might not refer to the date of composition but to the setting of the contents, being composed sometime after the events had taken place. This is more like the scenario since some of these psalms describe life-threatening situations, where composing a psalm in the heat of the moment would not have been a top priority. In many cases, these psalms include a thanksgiving section as well, showing that they were written after God had answered the prayers.

Message and purpose

There are myriad messages scattered through the 150 psalms, but overall, this record of the responses of God's people in worship and prayer serves the purpose of teaching us how to relate to God in various circumstances of life. The psalms also demonstrate God's sovereignty and goodness for his people in order to instill confidence in those who trust in him.

Contribution to the Bible

The relationship between God's activities in the life of his people and their responses to them is the most significant contribution of this book. God never spoke directly in any of these psalms as he often did in the narratives and the prophets. Therefore, they are written from the human's perspective as authors work their way through various life situations. The struggle to understand how God's attributes, particularly his sovereignty and goodness, relate to life's experiences is a major theme in the collection. These words are from a people who had not lost faith in God, although they might have been tempted to at times (Ps. 73). They wrestled with how God was dealing with them personally and as a community.

Structure

The book of Psalms is, from first to last, a book of poetry. Hebrew poetry lacks rhyme and regular meter but use parallelism wherein two (or three) lines are balanced and complete a thought. Some parallelism is synonymous, where the second line echoes the first. Antithetic parallelism uses a contrast between the two segments, and in synthetic parallelism, the second segment completes the idea in the first segment.

The Psalms can be divided into classes. There are hymns (145–150) and songs of thanksgiving (30–32). Psalms of lament (38–39) are prayers and cries to God on the occasion of distressful situations. Royal psalms (2, 110) are concerned with the early king of Israel. Enthronement psalms (96, 98) celebrate the kingship of Yahweh. Penitential psalms (32, 38, 51) express contrition and repentance, and wisdom or didactic psalms (19, 119) tend to be proverbial.

Outline

The book of Psalms is unlike most other biblical books since it contains many writings collected and compiled over a period of time and finally organized into its present form. For this reason, it is not possible to outline the book in the standard way. However, there is clearly a structure to the collection. The book is divided into five parts, also known as books. According to Jewish tradition, this fivefold divisions was based on the arrangement of the Torah, or Pentateuch, the first five books of the Bible. The book divisions are Book 1 (Pss. 1–41), Book 2 (Pss. 42–72), Book 3 (Pss. 73–89), Book 4 (90–106), and Book 5 (107–150).

Another part of the structure of the Psalms is that they are generally grouped together by their titles, such as those of Asaph and those of the sons of Korah. Following the close of each of the first four books is a doxology or statement identifying the end of the book and the beginning of another. The psalms containing these statements are known as "seam" psalms because they show "the piecing together" of these psalms to form the collection as it now stands.

Proverbs

Introduction

What is a proverb? Secular proverb seeks to state a general (not absolute) truth, such as "a fool and his money are soon parted." It is typically pithy; that is, it is brief but rich in meaning: "No pain, no gain." A proverb is practical; it gives advice that is useful in the real world: "A stitch in time saves nine." It should be applied; the reader should consider what changes he should make in his own life in light of the proverb: "Charity begins at home." A proverb is derived from astute observations about how life usually work; the creator of a proverb shows himself very knowledgeable and perceptive, able to see what is generally true and to draw conclusion from it: "The pen is mightier than the sword." In addition to all this, the proverbs in the book of Proverbs are also divinely inspired. Since they come from God, we know they are true, and we can be certain they are beneficial: "The one who understands a matter find success, and the one who trusts in the Lord will be happy" (16:20). Biblical proverbs not only offer practical advice for this life but also guide the reader to eternal life: "For the discerning the path of life leads upward, so that he may avoid going down to Sheol" (15:24).

Circumstances of writing

Author:

Solomon is credited with the proverbs in chapters 1–29 of the book of Proverbs (1:1, 10:1). There is biblical evidence that Solomon was wise and a collector of wise sayings (1 Kings 3:5–14; 4:29–34; 5:7, 12; 10:2, 3, 23–24; 11:41). Chapters 1–24 may have been written down during his reign 970–931 BC. The proverbs in chapters 25–29 were Solomon's proverbs collected by King Hezekiah who reigned in 716–687 BC (25:1). The last two chapters are credited to Agur and Lemuel (30:1, 31:1), about whom nothing else is known. An editor was inspired to collect the proverbs of Solomon, Agur, and Lemuel into the book that we have now.

Background

The reign of Solomon represented the peak of prosperity for the Israel nation. The period saw the greatest extent of the territory, and there was peace and international trade (1 Kings 4:20–25, 10:21–29). It is likely that Solomon knew about ancient tradition of wisdom in Egypt (1 Kings 3:1), but through inspiration and God's gift, he composed even better sayings (1 Kings 3:12; 10:6–7, 23). Solomon addressed his teaching to his son or sons, but these inspired wise sayings are applicable to all people. The book of Proverbs, like the rest of the Bible, contains stories, teaching, and examples. People should make appropriate application of these truths to their own situation (1 Cor. 10:11).

Message and purpose

Because these proverbs are in the Bible, they do not just entertain; they exhort, encourage, and offer hope. Solomon called readers, especially youth, to pursue wisdom rather than foolishness. He encouraged the inexperienced to become wise rather than mockers, to be teachable rather than incorrigible, to live rather than to die. He predicted that people who pursued wisdom would generally find success and happiness in this life, but he promised that they would absolutely find joy and blessing in eternity. There is a close connection between wisdom and God. For example, both prescribe obedience and morality, and both promise success and eternal life. They are connected because wisdom presupposes the fear of God; because

God is the source of this inspired, godly advice; and because God is the one who guarantees the blessings that wisdom promises. The benefits of wisdom and of God are the same. What wisdom promises is what God grants (4:4–8).

Structure

The book of Proverbs is in the wisdom genre. Wisdom books consist of the intelligent author's observations on the world and the people in it. However, without an inspired godly perspective, the world would be depressing and hopeless as parts of Job and Ecclesiastes show. Ultimately, biblical wisdom is informed by and founded on faith in God.

The process of observation, contemplation, and inspiration can be seen in Proverbs 24:30–34. After observing the deteriorated condition of "the field of a slacker" and "the vineyard of a man lacking sense," Solomon contemplated what he was seeing and was inspired: "I saw, and took it at heart; I looked, and received instruction" (v. 32). He either composed a new proverb or applied a familiar proverb to the situation: "A little sleep, a little slumber, a little folding of the arms to rest, and your poverty will come like a robber, your need, like a bandit" (vv. 33–34).

Proverbs is written as Hebrew poetry. Hebrew poetry is terse and concise. It uses a lot of imagery, and generally, the second line complements or contrasts the thought of the first. Contemplating how the second line relates to the first is a profitable way to meditate on a proverb.

In chapters 1–9, Solomon used imagery and sustained arguments to teach about the value of wisdom and the seduction of evil. In 22:17–24:34, there are "sayings" made up of several verses each, and in chapters 30–31, there are more sayings, including numerical sayings and alphabetic acrostic in praise of a capable wife. In the rest of the book, each proverb is generally one verse. Some scholars argue these individual proverbs are carefully arranged in groups, and each should be interpreted in the context of its group. Other scholars view the collection as unsystematic and argue that the immediate context seldom has any bearing on interpretation.

In either case, it is important to interpret any single proverb in the context of the book of Proverbs and the Bible as a whole. For example, while 21:14 may seem to encourage bribery, the rest of the book of Proverbs is clearly against it (15:27) as is the rest of Scripture (Exod. 23:8, Eccles. 7:7).

Outline

   I.   Solomon's exhortations and warnings (1:1–9:18)
      A. Contrast between wisdom and riches (1:1–3:20)
      B. Praise of wisdom, love, and worthy conduct (3:21–4:27)
      C. Warnings against lust, idleness, and deceit (5:1–7:27)
      D. A portrayal of wisdom (8:1–9:18)
  II. Solomon's proverbs (10:1–29:27)
      A. Collected proverbs (10:1–22:16)
      B. Thirty sayings of the wise (22:17–24:22)
      C. More sayings of the wise (24:23–34)
      D. Hezekiah's collection (25:1–29:27)
 III. Other proverbs (30:1–31:31)
      A. Words of Agur (30:1–33)
      B. Words of Lemuel (31:1–9)
      C. Praise of a capable wife (31:10–31)

Ecclesiastes

— ✍ —

Introduction

The Bible never shies about confronting painful truths or hard questions. The book Ecclesiastes faces the issue of how we can find meaning in life in light of the seemingly futile nature of everything. It will not allow the reader to retreat into superficial answers. It does not answer this problem by confronting us with hollow slogans. To the contrary, its motto is "everything is futile." But by forcing us to face the futility of human existence, it guides us to a life free of empty purpose and deceitful vindication.

Circumstances of writing

Author

According to 1:1–1:12, the author was David's son and a king over Israel from Jerusalem. Also, 12:9 speaks of the author as a writer of proverbs, so Solomon appears to be the author. Many scholars believe that Ecclesiastes was written too late in Israel's history for this to be true, and they want to date the book at least five hundred years after Solomon's time (later 450 BC). However, strong evidence attests that the book does not come from the age of Solomon. For instance, it displays great knowledge of literature from early Mesopotamia and Egypt.

One example is that the book shows an awareness of the "Harper's Song," poetry from Egypt that is much older than the age of Solomon. Ecclesiastes 9:7–9 is similar to that poetry, and it also resembles a portion of the famous *Epic of Gilgamesh* from Mesopotamia. It makes sense that Solomon, who had close contacts with Egypt and whose empire stretched up to the Euphrates River, would know and reflect on such texts. It is very doubtful that an anonymous Jew writing five hundred or more years later, when the Egyptians' and Mesopotamians' glory were finished and when Judah was a backwater nation, would have had access to these texts or could have understood them. By contrast, Ecclesiastes show no similarities to the Greek philosophy that flourished in the fifth century BC and later. All of these conditions point to the traditional view that Solomon authored the book.

Background

Ecclesiastes is wisdom literature, meaning it is the part of the Bible that is especially concerned with helping readers cope with the practical and philosophical issues of life. It has roots in the wisdom literature of Egypt and Babylon. Books like Proverbs and Ecclesiastes are the biblical answer to the search of truth. Proverbs is basic wisdom, giving the reader fundamental principles to live by. Ecclesiastes, by contrast, is for a more mature reader. It engages the question whether death nullifies all purpose and meaning in life.

Message and purpose

Ecclesiastes shows us that since we and our works are futile—that is, destined to perish—we must not waste our lives trying to justify our existence with pursuits that ultimately mean nothing. Put simply, Ecclesiastes examines major endeavors of life in light of the reality of death. The book warns us about the pursuit of several different purposes in life:

1. *Intellectual accomplishments.* Ecclesiastes affirms that wisdom helps us cope with life but denies that acquiring

knowledge as such is meaningful. Ultimately, the wise person and his works, like the fool and his deeds, perish.

2. *Wealth and luxury.* Wealth does not give life purpose. More than that, those who pursue riches waste their lives in bitterness, anxiety, and toil. Money does matter, and Ecclesiastes affirms that we need a strategy for maintaining a basic level of prosperity. But wealth of itself is a fraudulent substitute for true contentment.

3. *Politics.* Political power is inherently corrupting, and the worst evil in the world are committed by cruel and incompetent people in power. At the same time, government is necessary, and Ecclesiastes counsels the reader on how to survive in a world of political competition and thus how to have a stable, peaceful life.

4. *Religion.* Zeal for religion also comes in for criticism in Ecclesiastes. Its two warnings are that we should not try to impress God, and we should not wear ourselves out with irrational excess.

Positively, Ecclesiastes recommends that we do two things in light of the brevity of our days:

1. *Enjoy life.* This is not a philosophy of Hedonism, nor does it involve neglect of other duties because there is a time for everything under the sun. But a life without enjoyment is no life at all.

2. *Fear God.* This is an honest humility before God arising from an awareness of our weakness and sin. It includes awareness of our dependence on him and a remembrance of the fact that he is our Judge.

Contribution to the Bible

Ecclesiastes must be read with care because some of its verses, if read in isolation, seem to contradict other biblical teachings. It seems to deny the afterlife (3:18–22), to warn us against being too righteous (7:16), and to recommend a life of pleasure (10:19). But the real purpose of Ecclesiastes is to force us to take our mortality seriously and thus to consider carefully how we should live. Ecclesiastes knocks away all the facades by which we disguise the fact that life is short and we deny all our accomplishments will pass away. In this sense, Ecclesiastes anticipates the NT teaching that only God's grace, and no excessive zeal, saves us.

Structure

Ecclesiastes does not have the kind of structure we usually look for in a book of the Bible. At the first glance, it seems to move to and fro among various topics in a way that seems almost incoherent. It has no simple hierarchical outline, and it often jumps rapidly from one topic to the next. But a closer look reveals a structure that alternates between two perspectives: that of human existence apart from God and that of existence lived before God. If Ecclesiastes were music, it would be seen as antiphonal. The resolution of the tensions that permeate Ecclesiastes is found in the affirmation that the most important thing in life is to fear God and keeps his commands (12:13).

Outline

I. God and the futility of life (1:1–2:26)
   A. The humdrum of life (1:1–11)
   B. The teacher's quest (1:12–18)
   C. The emptiness of pleasure (2:1–3)
   D. The emptiness of possessions (2:4–11)
   E. The limits of wisdom (2:12–17)
   F. The emptiness of work (2:18–23)
   G. Pleasure, possessions, wisdom, and work in God's perspective (2:24–26)
II. Time and eternity (3:1–22)
   A. The rhythm of time (3:1–8)
   B. Eternity in time (3:9–15)
   C. Eternity and death (3:16–22)

III. Society (4:1–16)
  A. A place of injustice (4:1–6)
  B. A place of comfort (4:7–12)
  C. The more things change (4:13–16)
IV. Religion (5:1–6:12)
  A. Authentic religion (5:1–7)
  B. Wealth, God's perspective (5:8–6:12)
V. Wise sayings (7:1–29)
  A. A proverb (7:1–14)
  B. The value of moderation (7:15–22)
  C. Wisdom's limitations (7:23–29)
VI. Wisdom as prudence (8:1–10:20)
  A. Health (8:1)
  B. Authority figures (8:2–5)
  C. Timing (8:–7)
  D. Realistic expectations (8:8–9)
  E. Reverence for God (8:10–13)
  F. Iniquities (8:14)
  G. Enjoyment (8:15–9:10)
  H. Wisdom's limits (9:11–18)
  I. Wisdom preferable to folly (10:1–20)
VII. Invest in life (11:1–10)
VIII. Aging and death as teachers (12:1–8)
IX. The teacher's objectives and conclusion (12:9–14)

Song of Songs

Introduction

The Song of Songs celebrates the love of Solomon and his bride, who is called Shulamith, or the Shulammite (6:13). The excitement of courtship, the beauty of the wedding night, the sexuality of the first night and subsequent nights, as well as tender friendship—all of these elements make this book a celebration of romance and marital sensuality as God intended them to be.

Circumstances of writing

Author

The song claims authorship by Solomon in its title: "The Song of Songs which is Solomon's." The church has long accepted this at face value, but modern critics raise objections to Solomon as author. First, critics claim that the title did not originate with song but was added later by someone who wanted to attribute the work to the famous Solomon. However, no evidence supports the claim. Moreover, the structure of the book suggests that the title of the book is integral to the book's composition and is thus original. Like other biblical writers, the writer often structured content with attention to certain numbers—three, seven, and ten being some of the most common. Within the song, for example, the author designed seven sections (see below), a sevenfold praise (4:1–5), twice a tenfold praise (5:10–15, 7:1–5), and a tenfold occurrence of the abstract word for love (2:4–5, 7; 3:5; 5:8; 7:6; 8:4, 6–7). Apart from the title (1:1), he wove Solomon's name into six other places (1:5; 3:7, 9, 11; 8:11–12)—two in the last section, three in the central, and one in the first. With the inclusion of "Solomon" in the title, the name appears a perfect seven times and is symmetrically balanced with the song: twice in the first section balanced by twice in the last one, with three in the central. The title is thus as cleverly integrated with the lyrics as possible. It not only conforms to their melodic alliteration and meter, but it completes the sevenfold occurrence of Solomon in a manner that artistically balanced it throughout the song. In fact, the tenfold occurrence of "love" joins the sevenfold appearance of "Solomon" to show the song's subject and author. Hardly a later addition, the title seems to be original, constituting its first verse.

Another common objection to Solomon's authorship is the king's well-known 700 wives and 300 concubines (1 Kings 11:3). How could a man who lived like that write a song about devotion to one woman? It appears he could do so only because grace touched his heart. In this respect, he foreshadowed other biblical writers who, except for God's grace and calling, were the least qualified to write scripture. For example, Paul, the great apostle, wrote most eloquently of grace in his unworthiness (Tm 1:12–16). Solomon was a great man immersed in power and pleasure, but God opened his eyes to true love. Solomon also authored the book of Proverbs. Just as he did not always follow the precepts he recorded there, so he too evidently composed a great love song despite his failure to love in accordance with its ideals.

Background

A compelling historical reason to date the song as coming from the time of Solomon is its nearest literary parallel—the Egyptian love songs. No one doubts their origin prior to or contemporaneous with the time of Solomon, and the Egyptian love songs are indisputably the song's closest literary parallels.

Message and purpose

The central theme of the Song of Songs is a celebration of the goodness and beauty of romantic love. The song's romantic ideals are as captivating as its imagery: emotional intimacy, sensitive communication, delightful sexuality, profound companionship, common perspective, willing forgiveness, respect, integrity, security, love's devotion through the bleak season of winter, and love's renewal in new seasons of spring.

Since the song portrays perfect love, it is natural for the songwriter to compare it to the love of God for Israel. Solomon's love is like God's love for his people, and Shulamith's love is like a response from those people to God. If the NT will later tell us that a man's love for his wife should emulate Christ's love for his bride (Eph. 5:22–33), Solomon's song shows such a marriage patterned after divine love.

Since the song captures ideal love in its reflection of God's love for Israel, its romance also reflects the ideal love that God intended for a husband and a wife. We see a return to paradise in a courtship that blossomed in the uncluttered beauty of nature (1:15–2:3, 2:8–14), in a wedding night consummated with allusions to the garden of paradise (4:12–5:1), and in a marriage that delights in innocent lovemaking (4:1–5:1, 7:1–8:3).

The song's last praise of love captures all of this (8:5–7). The flames of love are like the fire of the Lord. In Genesis, God ruled over the waters of chaos to make the heaven and earth, creating in his image Adam and Eve to reflect his love in their union. In Exodus, God ruled over the deathly waters of the Red Sea to establish a new nation for his people. Since God's love is like fire (Deut. 4:24, 32:21–22) and since the love of Solomon and Shulamith recovers the innocence of Adam and Eve and reflects God's love for Israel, the song compares the power of romantic love to the eternal fire of God that no waters or rivers can quench.

Contribution to the Bible

A beautiful love song inspires us like grace, creating within us a desire for its beauty. Like such an enchanting love song, Solomon's song inspires a pursuit of the love it portrays. This romantic delight is not a modern fairy tale or fantasy from the past but reflects God's desire to form within us a pure and devoted love. We discover that there is bliss in married love that is reflective of the greater love believers experience as the bride of Christ. As this book's imagery informs us of romantic love, it also helps us anticipate the full consummation of our relationship with Christ when he returns for his bride.

Structure

The Song of Songs is a poem whose components form a chiastic structure. A chiasm takes the form

A

      B

           C

      B

A

Where *A* and *A* mirror each other and where the central element, *C*, conveys the main point of the poem. The outline below shows the structure of the Song of Songs. The author intended to emphasize the central elements of the structure, the day and night of the wedding (section V). When God inspired Solomon to write this song, he gave divine approval to romantic love.

The Hebrew text makes a distinction between the various speakers through a change in gender and number; the HCSB has added subheadings to clarify when the speakers change.

Structure and outline

I.   Section A—their story begins (1:2–2:7)
    A. Shulamith, Solomon, and the daughters of Jerusalem (1:1–4)
    B. Her brothers, their vineyards, and her appearance (1:5–6)

C. Her character and beauty (1:7–11)

D. Love's expression (1:12–2:5)

E. Refrain conclude Section A and begin Section B (2:6–7)

II. Section B—invitation to enjoy a spring day (2:6–17)

    A. Refrains of longing and patience (2:6–7)

    B. Her beloved's invitation to come from her house to enjoy spring (2:8–14)

    C. Refrains (after caution) of unity and invitation to her breasts (2:15–17)

III. Section C—night of separation preceding wedding (3:1–5)

    A. She awakened, alone and longing for him (3:1)

    B. Leaves home to find him (3:2)

    C. Is found by guards (3:3a)

    D. Asks for help (3:3b)

    E. Finds Solomon (3:4a)

    F. Returns home with him (3:4b)

    G. Is reunited with him through the night (3:4b), transition (3:5)

IV. Section D—wedding day and night (3:6–5:1)

    A. Songwriter's own words (3:6–11)

    B. Celebration of the wedding's beginning (3:6–11)

    C. Wedding night (4:1–5:1)

    D. Celebration of the wedding's consummation (5:1a)

    E. Songwriter's own words (5:1b)

V. Section C: Night of separation following wedding night (5:2–7:9)

    A. She is awakened, alone, and reluctant (5:2–8)

    B. Awakened to give tenfold praise (5:9–16)

    C. Aware of his presence in the garden (6:1–3)

    D. Receive his praise in the garden (6:4–10)

    C'. Recounts her journey to the garden (6:11–13)

    B'. Receives tenfold praise (7:1–5)

    A'. delightfully make love, together drift off to sleep (7:6–9)

VI. Section B': Invitation to enjoy a spring day (7:10–8:4)

    C'. Enjoyment of breasts and refrain of unity (7:7–8, 10)

B'. Her invitation to come enjoy spring then return to her house (7:11–8:2)

A'. Refrain and longing and patience (8: 3–4)

VII. Section A': Their story complete (8: 3–14)

E'. Refrains conclude section B' and begin section A' (8: 3–4)

D'. Love's devotion (8:5–7)

C'. Shulamith's character and beauty (8:8–9)

B'. Her brothers, their vineyards, and her appearance (8:10–12)

A'.Shulamith, Solomon, and shulamth's companions (8:13–14)

The design of the song underscores it central theme: a celebration of the goodness and beauty of romantic love.

Isaiah

Introduction

Isaiah was an eighth-century-BC prophet. His book is the first of the Prophets in the English canon and the first of the latter Prophets in the Hebrew canon. Isaiah is powerful in his poetic imagination, intriguing in its prophetic vision, and complex in its structure. One can never read or study the book without having new insights into the nature of God and our relationship with him. The author of the New Testament read the book of Isaiah in light of the coming Christ and realized that this prophet anticipated Messiah's coming with remarkable clarity. For this reason, they quoted Isaiah more than any other Old Testament book except the Psalms.

Circumstances of writing

Author:

The book presents itself as the writing of one man, Isaiah son of Amoz. The superscription to the book dates his prophetic activity as spanning the reigns of the kings of Judah: Uzziah (792–740 BC, is dated to this king's last year [6:1]), Jotham (740–735 BC), Ahaz (735–716 BC), and Hezekiah (716–686 BC). Not much is known about Isaiah apart from his prophecy.

Isaiah's authorship of the whole book has been vehemently contested in the modern period. Many scholars have argued that the historical Isaiah could not have written chapters 40–66. For those who believe that God knows the future and can reveal it to his servant, it is not problematic that God, through Isaiah, predicted the rise of Babylon, its victory against Judah, the exile, and return.

Background

Isaiah 6:1 records that Isaiah received his prophetic call in the last year of Uzziah's reign over Judah (ca. 740 BC). Uzziah's reign was a particularly prosperous time in Judah's history, but storm clouds were on the horizon. Assyria was on the rise again in the person of Tiglath-pileser III (745–727 BC). The Assyrian king threatened to engulf Syria and the northern kingdom of Israel. After Tiglath-pileser's death, his successors, Shalmaneser and Sargon, defeated the northern kingdom in 722 BC and deported its citizens. This event brought Judah even more under the shadow of the great empire. Isaiah 37:38 suggests that the prophet lived until Sennacherib's death in 681 BC.

Isaiah's vision extended beyond the eighth century, through the rest of the OT period and beyond. The NT authors cited Isaiah as finding fulfillment in the great events surrounding Jesus Christ, the Messiah and suffering Servant.

Message and purpose

Isaiah's message is relatively simple. First, Isaiah accused God's people of sin, rebelling against the One who made and redeemed them. Second, Isaiah instructed these sinners to reform their ways and act obediently. Third, Isaiah announced God's judgment on the people because of their sin. Finally, God revealed his future restoration of the people, or at least of the faithful remnant that survived the judgment. As part of the restoration of God's people, Isaiah foresaw both judgment on the nations (chs. 13–23) and a future turning of the nation to God (2:1–4). The first part of the book (chs. 1–39) emphasizes sin, the call to repentance, and judgment; the second part (chs. 40–66) emphasizes the hope of restoration. Other topics should be noted:

- *God the Holy One of Israel.* From the beginning to the end of the book, God is called the Holy One of Israel. At the time of Israel's call, the seraphim cried out "Holy, Holy, Holy is the Lord of Host" (6:3). God is set apart, completely removed from sin, the very epitome of moral perfection. God's people reflect the character of their Holy God according to the requirements of the Torah (Lev. 11:44–45, 19:2, 20:7), but they had fallen far short. Isaiah was commissioned to remind them of this high standard.
- *Trust and confidence.* Isaiah called God's people to trust God, and when they did not, he condemned them for it. They were to fear God, not other human beings. Most often. the Israelites betrayed God by trusting a powerful foreign nation or false gods.
- *God versus idols.* Because of the tendency of God's people to trust false gods, Isaiah's prophetic word often contrasted the true God with the false gods of the nation. God acted in history; idols did not. God could reveal the future; idols could not. God is eternal; idols were man-made and amounted to nothing.
- *Messiah and Servant.* Perhaps more than other parts of Isaiah, the passages describing a future anointed King (Messiah [9:1–7, 11:1–9]) and those describing the Servant (42:1–9, 49:1–6, 50:4–6, 52:13–53:12) have attracted the interest of Christian readers of the book. From the time of the NT, Christian readers have understood Jesus Christ as the ultimate fulfillment of the expectation of a future King and suffering Servant.

Structure

The book of Isaiah is a combination of both prose and poetry. The prose is found primarily in chapters 36–39, a section that forms a bridge between the two sections of the book (see message and purpose). Isaiah's poetry is rich and varied. He wrote hymns, wisdom poetry, and even poetry that resembles a love song (5:1–7). The richness is seen in Isaiah's vocabulary. He used over 2,200 different Hebrew words, far more variety than found in any other OT book.

Outline

I. Rebuke and promise from the Lord (1:1–6:13)
   A. Rebellion met with judgment and grace (1:1–31)
   B. Chastisement will bring future glory (2:1–4:6)
   C. Judgment and exile for the nation (5:1–30)
   D. Isaiah cleansed and commissioned (6:1–13)
II. The promise of Emmanuel (7:1–12:)
   A. Emmanuel rejected by worldly wisdom (7:1–25)
   B. God's deliverance and the coming Deliverer (8:1–9:7)
   C. Exile is coming for proud Samaria (9:8–10:4)
   D. Promise of a future glorious empire (10:5–12:6)
III. Coming judgment upon the nations (13:1–23:18)
   A. Babylon (13:1–14:23)
   B. Assyria (14:24–27)
   C. Philistia (14:28–32)
   D. Moab (15:1–16:14)
   E. Damascus and Syria (17:1–3)
   F. Israel (17:4–14)
   G. Cush (18:1–7)
   H. Egypt (19:1–20:6)
   I. Babylon additional judgment (21:1–10)
   J. Dumah (21:11–12)
   K. Arabia (21:13–17)
   L. Jerusalem (22:1–25)
   M. Tyre (23:1–18)
IV. First cycle of general judgment and promise (24:1–27:13)
   A. Universal judgment for universal sin (24:1–23)
   B. Praise to the Lord as Deliverer (25:1–12)
   C. A song of comfort for Judah (26:1–21)

D. Promise of preservation for God's people (27:1–13)

V. Woes upon the unbelievers of Israel (28:1–33:24)

   A. God's dealing with drunkards and scoffers (28:1–29)

   B. Judgment for those who try to deceive God (29:1–24)

   C. Confidence in man versus confidence in God (30:1–33)

   D. Deliverance through God's intervention (31:1–32:20)

   E. Punishment of deceivers and triumph of Christ (33:1–24)

VI. Second cycle of general judgment and promise (34:1–39:8)

   A. Destruction of the Gentile world powers (34:-17)

   B. The ultimate bliss of God's redeemed (35:1–10)

   C. Deliverance for King Hezekiah (36:1–39:8)

VII. Comfort for God's people (40:1–66:24)

   A. The purpose of peace (40:1–48:22)

   B. The Prince of peace (49:1–57:21)

   C. The program of peace (58:1–66:24)

Jeremiah

Introduction

The book and Prophet Jeremiah hold at least two great distinctions among all the Old Testament prophets: (1) this is the longest prophetic book in the Bible (with 1,364 verses); and (2) Jeremiah's life is more fully described than any of the other fifteen writing prophets. Into the tumultuous times of the last half of the seventh century and the first quarter of the sixth century BC came this prophet bearing a word from God for the stubborn people of Judah. The book's contents span roughly from 640 to 580 BC.

Circumstances of writing

Author

Jeremiah was a priest from the town of Anathoth (1:1). At the Lord's command, he neither married, nor had children because of the impending judgment that would come upon the next generation. His ministry as a prophet began in 626 BC and ended after 586 BC. He was a contemporary of Habakkuk and possibly Obadiah.

Background

The book of Jeremiah discusses the last days of Judah. King Hezekiah reigned for forty-two years (729–686 BC) and began to reverse Judah's spiritual bankruptcy. But Hezekiah's son, Manasseh, came to the throne. Idolatrous and superstitious cultic practices and rites came back like a flood. Manasseh's son Amon ruled for only two years (642–640 BC). He also reinstated idol worship as the official religion of Judah (2 Chron. 33:22–23).

Amon's eight-year-old son, Josiah, succeeded him on the throne. This lad walked in the ways of the former King David. When he was eighteen years old (622 BC), he called for long-delayed repairs to be made to the temple. During this work, a copy of the law of Moses was found. On the basis of hearing this word, the young king and all his people renewed the covenant with the Lord. However, this reformation failed to overcome the effects of the wickedness Manasseh and Amon had instituted.

Message and purpose

Jeremiah is the prophet of the "word of the lord" (1:2). Of the 349 times the OT uses the phrase "thus says the Lord," Jeremiah accounts for 157 of them. But this prophetic word that Jeremiah spoke was more than an objective revelation from God to the nation.

God's words were to be joy and food for Jeremiah's own soul. As 15:16 states, "Your words were found and I ate them. Your words were delight to me and the joy of my heart." However, God's words were sometimes a burden to the prophet. He sometimes grew tired of bringing God's message of judgment to an unresponsive people.

The people felt immune to any threat of divine judgment, but Jeremiah repeatedly warned them about the vanity of their reliance on ritual and external formalism. The prophetic word of God was to make the people blush and turn away from meaningless outward piety.

Contribution to the Bible

The best known passage in Jeremiah is the new covenant text in 31:31–34. Not only is it the largest OT text quoted in the NT (Heb. 8:8–12, 10:16–17) but arguably better than any other passage it links to God's ancient promises to Eve (Gen. 3:15), Abraham (Gen.

12:1–3), and David (2 Sam. 7:17–19) with NT assurances that God in Christ grants believers new hearts, salvation, and fellowship with him.

Structure

One date rings throughout the entire book of Jeremiah: "The fourth year of Jehoiakim son of Josiah king of Judah." That year, 605 BC, brought major change to the political situation of the near East. Both Egypt and Assyria were defeated at the battle of Carchemish (46:2–12; 2 Kings 24:7, 2 Chron. 35:20). Nebuchadnezzar ascended the throne of Babylon. In that same year, God instructed Jeremiah to put his prophecies into writing as a final test of King Jehoiakim's responsiveness to the word of God.

This significant dateline, "the fourth year of Jehoiakim," was placed at 25:1, 36:1, and 45:1, thereby dividing the prophet's book into three main sections: the prophet's faithfulness in carrying God's commission (chs. 2–24); the fierce opposition to his ministry (chs. 25–35); and the collapse of Judah (chs. 36–45).

The book of Jeremiah includes poetic sections (especially in chapters 2–25) and prose accounts as well. Critical scholars generally say that the poetry is Jeremiah's, and the prose is either the work of his friends or a person labeled a Deuteronomic writer (so designated because the prose sections are said to reflect the book of Deuteronomy). But we may ask, could not Jeremiah have written in both poetic and prose form? There is no reason to suppose he was incapable of writing in both forms.

Outline

   I.   Prologue—Jeremiah's call and vision (1:1–19)
   II.   Jeremiah calls for repentance (2:1–25:38)
       A.   Six early messages (2:1–20:18)
       B.   Four indictments on Israel's leadership (21:1–24:10)
       C.   Judgment against the nations (25:1–38)

III. Jeremiah stands firm despite harassment (26:1–36:32)
    A. The temple sermon repeated (26:1–24)
    B. The yoke of Babylon (27:1–22)
    C. The false prophet Hananiah (28:1–17)
    D. Letters to the exiles (29:1–32)
    E. The book of consolation/comfort (30:1–33:26)
    F. Judgment for Zedekiah (34:1–22)
    G. The obedience of the Rechabites (35:1–19)
    H. The writing and rewriting of the scroll (36:1–32)
IV. Jeremiah sees destruction ahead (37:1–45:5)
    A. Jeremiah and King Zedekiah (37:1–21)
    B. Jeremiah rescued by Ebed-melech (38:1–28)
    C. Jeremiah's fate at the fall of Jerusalem (39:1–18)
    D. Post-fall Judah and Governor Gedaliah (40:1–41:18)
    E. Jeremiah asked about going to Egypt (42:1–22)
    F. Jeremiah's counsel and God's word rejected (43:1–44:30)
    G. Summary—God's word to the scribe Baruch (45:1–5)
V. Prophecies against the nations (46:1–51:64)
    A. Egypt (46:1–28)
    B. The Philistines (47:1–7)
    C. Moab (48:1–47)
    D. The Ammonites (49:1–6)
    E. Edom (49:7–22)
    F. Damascus (49:23–27)
    G. Kedar and Hazor (49:28–33)
    H. Elam (49:34–39)
    I. Babylon (50:1–51:64)
VI. Epilogue—the fall of Jerusalem (52:1–34)

Lamentations

Introduction

This is a book about pain but with hope in God. The author vividly addresses the extremes of human pain and suffering as few other authors have done in history. For this reason, Lamentations is an important biblical source expressing the hard questions that arise during our times of pain. The suffering the author discusses was brought on by the brutal overthrow of Jerusalem in 586 BC, one of the darkest times in Jewish history.

Circumstances of writing

Author

Jeremiah's name has long been associated with this book. The Alexandrian form of the Greek Septuagint has these words preceding 1:1: "And it came to pass, after Israel had been carried away captive, and Jerusalem became desolated, that Jeremiah sat weeping, and lamented with this lamentation over Jerusalem." The Latin Vulgate adds this phrase: "and with a sorrowful mind, sighing and moaning, he said." The Talmud observes that Jeremiah wrote his own book and the book of Kings and Lamentation. Given this rich tradition linking Jeremiah to Lamentations, it seems safe to conclude he did indeed write the book.

Background

The sad background for these five poems of lament was the sacking of Jerusalem and the burning of the temple in 586 BC by the Babylonian army. Even though the book lists only one proper name ("Edom," 4:21–22), the allusions and historical connections to the events listed dramatically in 2 Kings 25, 2 Chronicles 36:11–21, and the book of Jeremiah are unmistakable. Perhaps a short list of the key events and some of their allusions in the book of Lamentations will help make this point.

Events in Lamentations:

1. Siege of Jerusalem (2:20–22; 3:5, 7)
2. Famine in the city (1:11, 19; 2:11–12, 19–20; 4:4–5)
3. Fight of the Judean army (1:3, 6; 2:2; 4:19–20)
4. Burning of the temple, place (2:3–5, 4:11, 5:18)
5. Breaching of the city walls (2:7–9)
6. Exile of the people (1:1, 4–5, 18; 2:9, 14; 3:2, 19; 42:22)
7. Looting of the temple (1:10, 2:6–7)
8. Execution of the leaders (1:15; 2:2, 20)
9. Vassal status of Judah (1:1, 5:8–9)
10. Collapse of expected foreign help (4:17, 5:6)

Message and purpose

Lamentations does not offer a complete understandable explanation for the suffering and pain found here, but it was important that the pain and suffering be connected to the actual events of 586 BC. If these pent-up feelings of agony could not be attached to some datable events, the pain could threaten to take on cosmic proportions. This is why history is necessary. When sorrow becomes detached from history, suffering gets out of hand because of lost perspective, tempting a suffering person to lose touch with reality. There was more than enough to weep over. The united laments of the people related to their covenant history with God. This anchored their sorrow but also gave their grief specific barriers, lest they should be overwhelmed and lose all hope.

Contribution to the Bible

Few things contrast religious and humanistic traditions more than their respective responses to suffering. The humanist sees suffering as a bare, impersonal event without ultimate meaning or purpose. For believers, suffering is a personal problem because they believe that all events of history are under the hand of a personal God. And if that is true, then how can God's love and justice be reconciled with our pain?

Lamentations gives no easy answers to this question, but it helps us meet God in the midst of our suffering and teaches us the language of prayer. Instead of offering a set of techniques, easy answers, or inspiring slogans for facing pain and grief, Lamentations supplies (1) orientation, (2) a voice for working through grief from "A to Z," (3) instruction on how and what to pray, and (4) a focal point on the faithfulness of God and the affirmation that he alone is our portion.

Structure

The book of Lamentations exhibits a remarkably fine artistic structure. Each of its five chapters (five poems) is a structurally unified text. The fact that there is an uneven number of poems allows the middle poems (ch. 3) to be the midpoint of the book. Thus, there is an ascent (or crescendo) up to a fixed climax for the entire book, thereby making chapter 3 central in its form and the message it imparts. Accordingly, the first two chapters form the steps leading up to the climax of 3:22–24, and from here, there is a descent in chapters 4 and 5.

The poems or songs of this book also exhibit the chiastic form (a crisscross inversion such as a-b, b-a). As such, chapters 1 and 5 are overall summaries of the disaster, 2 and 4 are more detailed descriptions of what took place, and chapter 3 occupies the central position.

Lamentations also utilizes the form of the alphabetic acrostic with the twenty-two-letter Hebrew alphabet. In chapter 5, each of its twenty-two stanzas consist of a single line, but this is the only chapter that is not an alphabetic acrostic. Chapter 3 is the most structured of the five poems.

Outline

I.   The city—an outside view (1:1–22)
   A.   Description of Jerusalem's afflictions (1:1–7)
   B.   Explanation of Jerusalem's afflictions (1:8–18)
   C.   Effect of Jerusalem's afflictions (1:19–22)

II. The wrath of God—an inside view (2:1–22)
   A.   Jerusalem's adversary (2:1–8)
   B.   Jerusalem's agony (2:9–16)
   C.   Jerusalem's entreaty (2:17–22)

III. The compassion of God—an upward view (3:1–66)
   A.   The rod of God's wrath (3:1–20)
   B.   The multitude of God's mercies (3:21–39)
   C.   The justice of God's judgments (3:40–54)
   D.   The prayer of God's people (3:55–66)

IV. The sins of all classes—an overall view (4:1–22)
   A.   The vanity of human glory (4:1–12)
   B.   The vanity of human leadership (4:13–16)
   C.   The vanity of human resources (4:17–20)
   D.   The vanity of human pride (4:21–22)

V.   The prayer—a future view (5:1–22)
   A.   Jerusalem invokes God's grace (5:1–18)
   B.   Jerusalem invokes God's glory (5:19–22)

Ezekiel

Introduction

The book of Ezekiel contains the divinely inspired prophecies of the prophet with the same name. These prophecies consist of oracles in the first person, giving the reader a sense of access to Ezekiel's private memoirs. Written primarily to the exile in Babylon, the prophecies equally emphasize judgment of sins and the promise of hope and restoration.

Circumstances of writing

Author

There is sufficient reason for maintaining that prophet Ezekiel composed the book of Ezekiel in Babylon. The work demonstrates such homogeneity and literary coherence that it's reasonable to conclude that all editorial work was carried out by a single person, the prophet himself.

The inclusion of historical dates at the beginning of many of the oracles and prophecies in Ezekiel is another important unifying factor. The book is one of the most chronologically ordered book of the Bible. Thirteen times a passage is included by an indication of time. The common point of orientation for the dates given in Ezekiel is the exile of king Jehoiachin of Judah in 598/597 BC. The occurrence of visions throughout the book (chaps 1:8–11:40–48) is another strong argument in favor of its overall unity. Finally, stylistic features throughout the book strengthen the unity argument.

Background

Ezekiel, son of Buzi, was among the approximately ten thousand citizens of Judah deported to Babylon when King Nebuchadnezzar invaded Jerusalem in 598/597 BC (2 Kings 24:10–17). His prophetic call came to him five years later (the fifth year of King Jehoiachin's exile), in 593. He received his call at the age of thirty (1:1), the year he should have begun his duties as a priest (Num. 4:3). The last dated oracle in the book occurs in the twenty-seventh year of King Jehoiachin (29:17), thus indicating that Ezekiel's ministry lasted twenty-two or twenty-three years. The prophet lived during the greatest crisis in Israel's history—the destruction of Jerusalem, its temple, plus the exile of Judah's leading citizens to Babylon.

Message and purpose

The message of the book revolves around the pivotal event in Israel's history—the fall of Jerusalem in 586 BC. Prior to the announcement of Jerusalem's fall, Ezekiel's message was characterized by judgment. In his scathing review of Israelite history, Ezekiel exposed the nation's moral depravity and absence of spiritual concern (2:1–8, 8:7–18, 13:1–23, 17:1–21, 20:1–32). After the destruction of Jerusalem was complete, and the nation was in exile, his message changed. He turned to a proclamation of hope, which is what the people now needed most. God would provide a new heart and a new spirit to enable the people to be faithful and avoid future judgment (11:17–20, 36:26–28). The Lord would establish a new temple (chs. 40–48) and a new way of worship for the people once they were restored.

The arrangement of the book (the announcement of judgment in the beginning and the declaration of restoration at the end) suggests that Ezekiel's message was ultimately one of hope and encouragement.

Six major theological statements are affirmed on Israel's behalf in the book:

1. The Lord will regather his scattered people (11:16–17, 16:1–63, 20:41, 34:11–13, 36:24, 37:21).
2. The Lord will bring the nation back to their land and will cleanse them from defilement (11:17–18, 20:42, 34:14–15, 36:24, 37:21).
3. The Lord will give his people a new heart and a new spirit so they might walk in his ways (11:19–20, 16:62, 34:30–31, 36:25–28, 37:23–24).
4. The Lord will restore the Davidic dynasty (34:23–24, 37:22–25).
5. The Lord will bless Israel with unprecedented prosperity and security in their land (34:24–29, 36:29–30, 37:26).
6. The Lord will establish his permanent residence in the midst of Israel (37:26–28, 40:1–48:35). All the covenants made with Israel will be fulfilled when she is restored to the promised land and messianic kingdom is established.

Contribution to the Bible

There are not many quotations of the book of Ezekiel in the NT, but there are some notable correlations. For instance, the structure of the book of Revelation, which begins with a vision of Christ, corresponds to the appearances of God in Ezekiel's visions. The end of the book of Revelation also reflects the end of Ezekiel where the river flows from the presence of God (Ezek. 47:1–12, Rev. 21:1–22:6). Finally, the depiction of the return of the exiles as resurrected from the dead is analogous to Paul's concept of regeneration (Eph. 2:5).

Structure

The Prophet Ezekiel displayed a distinct style throughout his prophetic work. The phrase "son of man" occurs ninety-three times as a title for Ezekiel, focusing on the prophet's human nature. The expression "the hand of the Lord was on me," which is said elsewhere only of Elijah (1 Kings 18:46) and Elisha (2 Kings 3:15), occurs in the various major sections of Ezekiel (13; 3:22; 33:22; 37:1). The so-called recognition formula that you (or they) "may know that I am Yahweh," a characteristic phrase of the exodus narrative (Exod. 6:6–8; 7:5; 10:1–2; 14:4, 18), occurs about sixty times in Ezekiel. The introductory oracle phrase "the word of the Lord came to me" occurs forty-six times in the book and alerts the reader to the beginning of a separate section. The phrase "I, Yahweh, have spoken" also occurs frequently in Ezekiel (5:13, 15, 17; 17:21, 24; 21:17, 32; 22:14; 24:14; 26:14; 30:12; 34:24; 36:36; 37:14). Another feature for which Ezekiel is well-known is his performance of symbolic, dramatic actions. Account of this method of communication occur throughout the book. He also used the literary technique of allegory to communicate his prophecies. His allegories include Jerusalem as a vine (ch. 15) and majestic eagle (17:1–21), the Davidic dynasty as a lioness (19:1–9) and a vineyard (19:10–14), a sword as judgment (21:1–17), and Oholah and Oholibah as corrupt sisters (23:1–35).

A final characteristic of the book is the citation of previously written scripture in Ezekiel's prophecies. This is evident in the judgment oracles of chapters 4–5 that depend heavily on the curses listed in Leviticus 26. Ezekiel also references other portions of canonical scripture, including Numbers 18:1–7, 22–23 (in Ezek. 44:9–16) and Zephaniah 3:1–4 (Ezek. 22:25–29).

Outline

    I.   Israel, a rebellious house, will fall (1:2–24:27)
        A.   Ezekiel sent as God's spokesman (1:1–3:27)
        B.   First series of symbolic actions (4:1–7:27)
        C.   Vision of Israel's doom (8:1–11:25)
        D.   Second series of symbolic actions (12:1–14:23)
        E.   Parables of doom (15:1–19:14)
        F.   Rebukes and threats (20:1–22:31)
        G.   Two final parables and last symbolic action (23:1–24:24)

       H. News of the fall of the rebellious house (24:25–27)

II. Pagan foreign nations will be destroyed (25:1–32:32)
       A. Amon (25:1–7)
       B. Moab (25:8–11)
       C. Edom (25:12–14)
       D. Philistia (25:15–17)
       E. Tyre (26:1–28:19)
       F. Sidon (28:20–26)
       G. Egypt (29:1–32:32)

III. Disciplined Israel will be destroyed (33:1–48:35)
       A. Basis of this message of hope (33:1–20)
       B. News of Jerusalem's fall arrives (33:21–33)
       C. The promises of restoration (34:1–39:29)
       D. The vision of restoration (40:1–48:35)

Daniel

— ❦ —

Introduction

Daniel, whose name means "God judges" or "God's judge," was a
sixth-century-BC prophet living in exile in Babylon. Daniel recounts
key events firsthand that occurred during the Jewish captivity and
also shares visions that were given to him by God.

Circumstances of writing

Author

The critical view of the book of Daniel suggests it was written by a second-century-BC Jewish author, not the historical Daniel.
This view is largely based on a naturalistic perspective that denies
the possibility of the authentic foretelling found in Daniel. On the
other hand, the traditional view maintains that Daniel the prophet
did indeed write the book sometime shortly after the end of the
Babylonian captivity (sixth century BC). Internal testimony supports
the claim. In the text itself, Daniel claimed to have written down
visions given by God (8:2; 9:2, 20; 12:5). Passages which contain
third-person references to Daniel do not disprove his authorship.
After all, authors commonly refer to themselves in the third person
as, for instance, Moses does in the Pentateuch. Moreover, God speaks
of himself in the third person (Exod. 20:2, 7). The prophet Ezekiel
referred to Daniel several times (Ezek. 14:14, 20; 28:3), a promi-

nence that would benefit the writing prophet. Finally, Jesus Christ attributed the book to Daniel himself (Matt 24:15, Mark 13:14).

Background

The historical setting of the book of Daniel is the Babylonian captivity. The book opens after King Nebuchadnezzar's first siege of Judah (605 BC) when he brought Daniel and his friends to Babylon, along with other captives among the Judean nobility. Nebuchadnezzar assaulted Judah again in 597 and brought ten thousand captives back to Babylon. In 586, he once again besieged Jerusalem, this time destroying the city, the holy temple, and exiling the people of Judah to Babylon. Daniel's ministry began in 605 when he arrived at Babylon with the first Jewish captives, extended throughout the Babylonian captivity (which ended in 539), concluded sometime after the third year of Cyrus the Great, the Medo-Persian king who overthrew Babylonia (see Dan. 1:21 and 10:1).

When was the book written? While the critical view maintains a date of 165 BC in the Maccabean period primarily because of the precise prophecies related to that time, the traditional view asserts that it was written just after the end of Babylonian captivity in the late sixth century BC. The book contains a factual recounting of events from Daniel's life, supernatural prediction of events that took place during the intertestamental period, and prophecies that are yet to be fulfilled.

Manuscript evidence supports the early date. Fragments from Daniel were found among the Dead Sea Scrolls, a collection that included other books of the Bible that were written well before the second century. Linguistic evidence demonstrates that the use of Aramaic in Daniel fits a fifth- to sixth-century-BC date because it parallels the Aramaic of Ezra as well as the *Elephantine Papyri* and other secular works of that period. Historical evidence also supports the early date. For example, Daniel accurately described Belshazzar as coregent with another king (Nabonidus), a fact that was not known until modern times. In summary, the late-date view is driven by a presuppositional rejection of supernatural prophecy and not objective evidence.

Message and purpose

The theme of the book of Daniel is the hope of the people of God during the times of the Gentiles. The phrase "the times of the Gentiles" used by Jesus (Luke 21:24) refers to the time between the Babylonian captivity and Jesus's return. It is a time when God's people was under ungodly world dominion. The book promotes hope by teaching that all the time, "the Most High God is ruler over the kingdom of men" (5:21). Daniel's purpose was to exhort Israel to be faithful to the sovereign God of Israel during the times of the Gentiles. He accomplished this by examples of godly trust and prophecies of God's ultimate victory.

Contribution to the Bible

Daniel's book establishes the validity of predictive prophecy and lays the foundation for understanding end-times prophecy, especially the book of Revelation in the NT. But most importantly, it emphasizes that the Lord has dominion over all the kingdoms of the earth, even in evil days when wicked empires reign. Two key words in the book are *king* (used 183 times) and *kingdom* (used 55 times). Above all, Daniel teaches that the God of Israel is the Sovereign of the universe, "for His dominion is an everlasting dominion, and His kingdom is from generation to generation" (4:34).

Structure

The genre of the book of Daniel is narrative, recounting historical events for the purpose of present and future instruction. The narrative contains history, prophecy, and apocalyptic visions. Apocalyptic literature refers to revelation by God given through visions and symbols with a message of eschatological (end-time) triumph.

Although Daniel contains apocalyptic elements, it is not an apocalyptic book. Rather, it is a narrative that includes apocalyptic visions.

Noting that the book of Daniel contains both history (chs. 1–6) and prophecy (chs. 7–12), some divide the book into two sections. A better way to see the book's structure is based on the two languages it uses: 1:1–2, Hebrew; 2:4–7:28, Aramaic; and 8:1–12:13, Hebrew. The Hebrew sections pertain primarily to the people of Israel, which is fitting since Hebrew was Israel's national language. Aramaic was the international language of that time. Fittingly, the Aramaic section of Daniel demonstrates God's dominion over the international Gentile nations.

Outline

I.   Godly remnant in the times of the Gentiles (1:1–21)
  A. Daniel and his friends in the Babylonian captivity (1:1–7)
  B. Daniel and the king's food (1:8–16)
  C. Daniel and the Lord's reward (1:17–21)
II. God's sovereignty over the times of the Gentiles (2:1–7:28)
  A. Daniel and the king's dream (2:1–49)
  B. Daniel's friends and the fiery furnace (2:1–49)
  C. Nebuchadnezzar's pride, madness, and repentance (4:1–37)
  D. Belshazzar's feast and the writing on the wall (5:1–30)
  E. Daniel in the lions' den (6:1–28)
  F. Daniel's vision of the four beasts, the ancient day, and the Son of man (7:1–28)
III. God's people in the times of the Gentiles (8:1–12:13)
  A. Daniel's vision of the ram and the male goat (8:1–27)
  B. Daniel's prayer and vision of the seventy weeks (9:1–27)
  C. Daniel and his final visions (10:1–12:13)

Hosea

Introduction

Hosea is one of the most autobiographical of the prophetic books in that the opening account of Hosea's own marriage and family form a vital part of his unique message. God's word and grace and his call to repent are dramatically portrayed and punctuated by Hosea's scorned but constant love for his wife, Gomer, and by the odd names of his three children. Apart from this information about his immediate family, hardly anything is known about Hosea. His divinely commissioned marriage to the promiscuous Gomer, which brought Hosea such heartache, seems to have been the beginning of his long career. But rather than ministering in spite of personal sorrow, his troublesome marriage was the foundation stone of his ministry.

Circumstances of writing

Author

According to the first verse, Hosea's prophetic career spanned at least forty years. It began sometime during the reign of Jeroboam II, who ruled Israel, the northern kingdom, as coregent with his father, Jehoash, from 793 to 782 BC, then independently until 753 BC. Hosea's ministry ended sometime during the reign of Hezekiah, who ruled Judah from 716 to 686 BC.

Although the southern kingdom of Judah was not neglected in Hosea's prophecy (e.g., 1:7, 11; 6:11; 12:2), his messages were directed primarily to the northern kingdom of Israel, often referred to as Ephraim (5:3, 12–14; 6:4; 7:1), and represented by the royal city, Samaria (7:1; 8:5–6; 10:5, 7; 13:16). Hosea apparently lived and worked in or around Samaria, probably moving to Jerusalem at least by the time Samaria fell to the Assyrians in 722 BC.

Background

The reign of Jeroboam II, the northern kingdom's greatest ruler by worldly standards, was a time of general affluence, military might, and national stability. The economy was strong, the future looked bright, and the mood of the country was optimistic, at least for the upper class (Hosea 12:8, Amos 3:15; 6:4–6). Syria was a constant problem to Israel, but Adad-nirari III of Assyria had brought Israel relief with an expedition against Damascus, the Syrian capital, in 805 BC.

Then after Adad-nirari's death in 783 BC. Israel and Judah expanded during a time of Assyrian weakness (the time of Judah). But after Jeroboam's death in 753 BC, Israel sank into near anarchy, going through six kings in about thirty years, four of whom were assassinated (Zechariah, Shallum, Pekahiah, and Pekah). Since Assyria also regained power during this time, Israel was doomed. Of course, the real reason Israel crumbled was God's determination to judge the people for their sins as Hosea and Amos made clear. Most of Hosea's messages were probably delivered during these last thirty years of Israel's nationhood.

Message and purpose

Indictment. According to Hosea, Israel sinned in four ways. First, they were violating basic covenant requirements of faithfulness and kindness, rejecting God's knowledge and his law. They had become self-satisfied and proud and had forgotten God's grace. They even spoke contemptuously against him. Second, they were engaging in idolatry harlotry, or cult prostitution. Third, they were trusting in human devices (kings, princes, warriors, and foreign covenants) rather than God. Finally, they were guilty of injustice and violence, including murder, theft, lying, and oppression of the defenseless.

Instruction. Through Hosea, the Lord told the people of Israel to stop their promiscuity, idolatry, and iniquity and return to him in humility and faithfulness toward the law of the covenant.

Judgment. Hosea informed Israel that their present distress was because the Lord had abandoned them and that further discipline would come. This would include foreign domination, exile, destruction, desolation, and death.

Hope. Hosea reminded Israel of the Lord's grace and love in making them a people and in blessing them in the past with his attentive and patient care and his abundant provision. He was their only hope, and his ways were right. The Lord also assured them that in response to their repentance and faith, he would again have compassion on them and redeem them. He would remove unrighteousness and restore the covenant, bringing righteousness and the knowledge of God, and He would rebuild and beautify Israel.

Structure

The first three chapters of the book establish a parallel between the Lord and Hosea. Both were loving husbands of unfaithful wives. Hosea's three children, whose names served as messages to Israel, represent an overture to the second main division of the book which presents it accusations and the call to repent in groups of three. Just as chapter 1 (a third-person account of Hosea's family) is balanced by chapter 3 (a first-person account), so the final main division of the book alternates between first-person announcements of God's message and third-person reports from the prophet.

Contribution to the Bible

Hosea compared the relationship between God and his people to that of a husband and his wife, drawing a parallel between spiritual and marital unfaithfulness. The Bible is very clear in its moral code that sexual act can legitimately take place within the context of the marriage relationship. Thus the image of marriage and sex, a relationship that is purely exclusive and allows no rivals, is an ideal image of the relationship between God and his people (*Dictionary of Biblical Imagery*, p. 778).

Yet nothing can quench God's love for his covenant people. Like a marriage partner, God is deeply involved in our lives and in pain when we go our way. God demands love and loyalty from his own. Often, God's people have failed to demonstrate wholehearted love for him. But he stands ready to forgive and restore those who turn to him in repentance. In buying Gomer's freedom, Hosea pointed ahead to God's love perfectly expressed in Christ, who bought the freedom of his bride, the church, with his own life.

Outline

    I.   The pain and persistence of divine love (1:1–3:5)
         A.   God's message to Israel through Hosea's family (1:1–2:23)
         B.   Hosea's testimony to his restored marriage (3:1–5)
    II.   Threefold accusation and call to repent (4:1–7:16)
         A.   Indictment and warning (4:1–5:15)
         B.   Call to repent and God's grief at Israel's refusal (^;1–7:16)
    III. Alternating lament of the Lord and Hosea (8:1–14:9)
         A.   Failure of false hopes (8:1–10:15)
         B.   Israel's punishment for rebellion (11:1–13:16)
         C.   Final call to repent (14:1–9)

Joel

Introduction

The book of Joel is one of the shortest in the Old Testament. The first part (1:1–2:17) describes a terrible locust plague concluding with a plea for confession of sins. The second part (1:18–3:21) proclaims hope for the repentant people coupled with judgment upon their enemies.

Circumstances of writing

Author

Joel (means "Yahweh is God") is identified as the son of Pethuel. He is not easily identified with the other Joels of Scripture (1 Sam. 8:2; 1 Chron. 4:35, 6:33, 11:38, 15:7; Ezra 10:43; Neh. 11:9), leaving us only his book to know him, his calling from God, and his work. The book itself gives no biographical information other than his father's name.

Background

Dating the book of Joel has always been difficult and mainly conjecture, with suggestions ranging as widely as premonarchial Israel to the postexile period, sometimes well into the Hellenistic period.

Message and purpose

What is striking about the book of Joel is that it has no indictment section listing the offenses of the people. The only clue as what sins called forth the prophet's message is found in the instruction of 2:12–13 to repent, that is, "to turn to with all your heart" and "tear your hearts, no just your clothes." All the other prophets (except Jonah, who does not use the prophetic genre) have at least some explicit indication of what behavior needed to be changed. Joel was concerned mainly with motivation, with messages of judgment and hope.

There are many exhortations in the book, but they are almost all formal rather to hear (1:2–3), to war (2:1, 3:9–13), to lamentation (1:5, 8, 11, 13–14; 2:15–16, though some interpreters understand these as indirect calls for repentance), and to celebration (2:21–23). The only true instruction message in Joel occurs in 2:12–13, the call to repentance.

Joel's message was concerned primarily with motivating repentance by proclaiming the day of the Lord, which is "at the same time one event and many events" and "refers to a decisive action of Yahweh to bring His plan for Israel to completion" (D. A. Garrett). The locust plague is understood as judgment from God and a harbinger of the day of the Lord (1:2–20, especially v. 15). Then Joel announced that a worse judgment was coming through a human army (2:1–11). This is also called the day of the Lord (2:1, 11).

Joel insisted that the only hope for God's people was through repentance (2:12–17). He assured Judah that repentance would be rewarded with physical (2:18–27) and spiritual (2:28–32) restoration associated with the day of the Lord (2:31). He concluded by promising a day of Lord that would bring judgment against nations opposing the Lord and his people (3:14).

Locusts. The book of Joel contains four specific words translated "locusts" in English. In both 1:4 and 2:25, "locusts" is modified by four different adjectives: "devouring," "swarming," "young," and "destroying." Interpreters have longed to know what relationship exists between the locusts and the army that is mentioned later in

Joel. Are they distinct from each other? Is one a metaphor for the other? Or are they two aspects of God's judgment against Israel and the nations? Are the locusts actual, metaphorical, or typological?

It is important to note that both the army of invading locusts and the foreign army came as judgment of God. Also, locusts can be described as invading army, and an army of men could apply to be called a plague of destructive locusts.

The Day of the Lord. The phrase "Day of the Lord" figures prominently in the book of Joel. This describes the judgment day of God. That judgment could be directed both against the nation of Israel and against the "nations." The specific phrase occurs in the OT in Isaiah 13:6, 9; Ezekiel 13:5; Joel 1:15, 2:1, 11, 3:14; Amos 5:18, 20; Obadiah 15; Zephaniah 1:7, 14; and Malachi 4:5. The concept itself may also be found in Jeremiah 46:10 and several other passages.

The "Day of the Lord" has several adjectives attached to it: "darkness and not light" (Amos 5:18, 20), "great and awesome" (Mal. 4:5), "great and remarkable" (Acts 2:20). Associated with it are cosmic calamities; the sun will be turned to darkness and the moon to blood (Acts 2:20, Rev. 6:12).

Extended descriptions of the Day of the Lord are found in Isaiah 13, 34; Ezekiel 7; and Joel 2. In Ezekiel 7, we find that the Lord will send his anger against the land of Israel and judge it according to its ways. He will punish it for all its abominations. Disasters are coming, one after another. The judgment theme is prominent in Joel, as is the idea that the day is near when God will make himself known through his judgments. In a move that shocked the Hebrews, God brought the most evil nations to take possession of Judah and Israel.

Contribution to the Bible

The book of Joel shows us the Creator and Redeemer God of all the universe in complete control of nature. Joel made it clear that the God of judgment also is a God of mercy who stands ready to redeem and restore when his people come before him in repentance. Joel points to a time when the Spirit of God would be present upon all people. On the day of Pentecost, Peter proclaimed that the new day of Spirit-filled discipleship, foretold by Joel, had arrived (Acts 2:17–21).

Structure

Joel's use of repetition gives the book the appearance of a series of folding doors, in some cases doors within doors. As Garrett has shown, the overall structure balances the section on God's judgment through the locust plague (1:1–20) with a section on the land's physical restoration (2:21–27). The prophecy of an invading army (2:1–11) is balanced by a prophecy on the destruction of this army (2:20). In the center is the highly prominent call to repent and the promise of renewal (2:12–19). But this balanced structure overlaps with another. The prophecy of the destruction of the invading army (2:20) is also balanced with the final prophecy of the Lord's vengeance against all the nations (3:1–21). Finally, the assurance of the land's physical restoration through rain (2:21–27) is balanced by the promise of the people's spiritual restoration through the outpouring of God's Spirit (2:28–32).

Outline

    I.   The locust plague (1:1–20)
    II.   An invading northern army (2:1–11)
    III. Repentance and renewal (2:12–19)
    IV. Northern army destroyed (2:20)
    V.   Physical restoration of the land (2:21–27)
    VI. Spiritual revival of the people (2:28–32)
    VII. Vengeance on the nations (3:1–21)

Amos

―――――――― ❦ ――――――――

Introduction

Amos is the first of the four eighth-century-BC prophet, which also included Hosea, Isaiah, and Micah. Along with Hosea, Amos's ministry was to Israel even though he was from Judah. He was a layman who did not consider himself a professional prophet (7:14–15). Through words and visions, Amos spoke against the superficial religious institutions of his day.

Circumstances of writing

Author

Amos was a shepherd from Tekoa, a village about ten miles south of Jerusalem. He received a call from God to the north to prophesy against Samaria and the kingdom of Israel, probably around 760 BC. We do not know how long he actually was in the north; it appears to have been a fairly short time. He provoked a great deal of opposition and anger as illustrated by his encounter with Amaziah, the priest of Bethel (7:10–17). Apparently, he wrote his book, a summary of his prophecies, after his return to Judah. He probably wrote it with the aid of a scribe.

Background

Amos prophesied during the reign of Uzziah of Judah (792–740 BC) and Jeroboam II of Israel (793–753 BC). This was a time of great prosperity and military success for both nations as all their traditional enemies were in a weakened condition. Samaria, the capital city of Israel, enjoyed enormous wealth, and luxuries flowed into the city.

At the same time, decades of struggle with Damascus had left the population exhausted. Many farmers were reduced to poverty. Their more affluent neighbors, and especially the aristocracy, swooped in with loans that the poor could not repay and then reduced the debtors to slavery and seized their lands. The leaders of society believed they have no reason to fear for the future. Their city had high walls and fortified citadels, and their army were everywhere, victorious. They were the chosen people of God, and they considered themselves immune from judgment.

Message and purpose

Several key teachings make up the message of Amos:

1. God is impartial and fair, judging each nation appropriately. Neither Jew, nor Gentile is exempted from divine judgment. The Gentiles are punished for moral outrages that we would now call "crimes against humanity," while the Jews are judged by the demands of the Mosaic law (1:3–2:3; cp. with 2:4–5).
2. God despises human pride, especially when it is demonstrated through confidence in military power, wealth, and indifference toward other people (6:1–8).
3. God is especially harsh against anyone who abuses or cheats the poor (8:4–6).
4. God is not impressed by worship services with music and celebration if the people have unrepentant hearts (4:4–5; 5:21–24).
5. Religious leaders who oppose genuine work of God are subject to special judgment (7:10–17).

6. People who are blinded by their confidence in their special status before God assume that they have no reason to fear divine judgment, but they are totally misguided (5:18–20).

7. When troubles begin to mount up against a nation, the people should see this as a warning from God and repent before it is to late (4:6–12).

8. Even after judgment, when it seems that all hope is lost (9:1–4), God is able to bring redemption and salvation (9:13–15).

9. Israel's hope (and humanity's hope) is in the line of David, which God will raise up to establish his kingdom (9:11–12). We now know that this hope is fulfilled in David's descendant, Jesus Christ.

Contribution to the Bible

Amos reminds us of the sovereignty of God in his involvement with his people. God will bring his judgment, a reality that certainly came to pass. Amos's emphasis on the Day of the Lord had implications for Amos's contemporaries, but it also reminds the modern reader of a coming day referred to repeatedly in the NT—the day of Christ's return.

Structure

After the superscript (1:1), the book of Amos is divided into seven parts. The first part, the introduction, is a single verse (1:2). This is followed by six major divisions—1:3–2:16, 3:1–15, 4:1–13, 5:1–6:14, 7:1–8:3, 8:4–9:15. Remarkably, formulas of divine speech (statements such as "the Lord says," "the Lord has spoken," and "the Lord's declaration" are evenly distributed in these sections. Amos 1:3 to 2:16 has fourteen such formulas, and each of the following sections have seven each, for a total of forty-nine. The basic structure and content of each section is described in the notes.

Outline

I. Prophecies against the nations (1:1–2:16)
    A. Superscription and proclamation (1:1–2)
    B. Indictment of neighboring nations (1:3–2:3)
    C. Indictment of Judah (2:4–5)
    D. Indictment of Israel (2:6–16)
II. Three discourses against Israel (3:1–6:14)
    A. A declaration of judgment (3:1–15)
    B. The depravity of (4:1–13)
    C. A lamentation for Israel's sin and doom (5:1–6:14)
III. Symbolic visions of Israel's condition (7:1–9:10)
    A. Devouring locusts (7:1–3)
    B. A flaming fire (7:4–6)
    C. A plumb line (7:7–17)
    D. A basket of ripe fruit (8:1–14)
    E. The Lord at the altar inflicting discipline (9:1–10)
IV. Promises of Israel's restoration (9:11–15)

Obadiah

Introduction

Many prophetic books contain prophecies against several nations, but the book of Obadiah focuses exclusively on the nation of Edom. Obadiah's short message centers on the approaching Day of the Lord and the promise that Israel will possess the land of Edom.

Circumstances of writing

Author

Presumably, Obadiah (v. 1) was the author of the book, but nothing else is known about him. His common Hebrew name, denoting "servant of the Lord," is shared by at least a dozen persons in the Old Testament.

Background

The time of writing of Obadiah is disputed, with a wide variety of proposed dates from the tenth to the fifth centuries BC, depending on when the invasion and plunder of Jerusalem (vv. 11–14) occurred. The two most popular views are during the reign of King Jehoram of Judah (ca. 848–841 BC) and shortly after the final destruction of Jerusalem by the Babylonians (587–586 BC).

The former date (ca. 845 BC) was when the Philistines and Arabs plundered Judah (2 Chron. 21:16–17), and the Edomites revolted (2 Kings 8:20), presumably then becoming allies of the invaders. Since the text does not explicitly indicate the cooperation of the Edomites with the Philistines and Arabs, the latter date (mid-sixth or even fifth century BC) fits the biblical data better, including Obadiah 20 (the dispersed exiles of the Israelites and of Jerusalem to be restored, as opposed to dates before the dispersion of Israel, by 722 BC, or of Judah, 605–586 BC).

This postexilic view is also supported by the mention of the Edomite involvement in Jerusalem's downfall (Obad. 10–14, gloating over the fall of Jerusalem, as in other sixth-century-BC texts—Lam. 4:21a, Ezek. 35:15; cp. Lam. 2:15–17—and participating in the plunder) which would result in the Lord's promised justice ("as you have done, so it will be done to you" on their heads, Obad. 15).

Message and purpose

Judgment on Edom's arrogant presumption. Yahweh's judgment was predicted for Edom because of her arrogance in trusting geographical security (vv. 3–5), diplomatic treaties (v. 7), and the counsel of her famed wise men (v. 8, Jer. 49:7) instead of the true God of Israel. Edom was doubly deceived, depending on their own human understanding (Obad. 3, 8) and believing in the loyalty of their human allies (v. 7). Thus God would bring them down from the lofty cliffs and caves of their mountains. He would cover the Edomites with shame because of their arrogant gloating and gleeful participation in the downfall of their brother, Jacob, the nation of Judah (vv. 10–14).

The Day of the Lord. Obadiah spoke of the nearness of the Day of the Lord (Isa. 13:6; Joel 1:15, 2:1; Zeph. 1:7, 14), focusing on the darkness and gloom of Yahweh's wrath (Isa. 13:6–13; Joel 1:15, 2:1–3, 10–11, 31; Zeph. 1:7–18, 2:2; Mal. 4:1–3, 5). He emphasized the dual nature of the Day of the Lord in bringing retributive judgment on the historical nation Edom and "Edom" as symbolic of Israel's archenemies (payback on their heads; Obad. 15) while, at the same time, bringing salvation (or restoration) for the nation of Israel (Joel 2:30–32; Zeph. 2:1–10, 3:8–16). In the OT, Edom was a historical entity whose people may have been completely wiped out by AD 70 (see notes at Obad. 3, 10, 18). This historical entity blends with Edom, a symbol for Israel's end-time enemies (cp. vv. 15–16; Isa. 63:1–6; Ezek. 35, 36:2, 5—the context of the Day of the Lord against all the nations).

Israel's repossession of the land (vv. 17–21). In the second conquest motif, the Hebrew word meaning "possess by dispossessing" is used five times: four times of Israel (both north and south) dispossessing (v. 17) the inhabitants of the promised land (vv. 19–20) and once the same root (v. 17) describes those enemies (including Esau) who had dispossessed them. Reminiscent of the conquest of Canaan, the Hebrew word was often used in Deuteronomy of God's instructions for conquering the promised land (Deut. 1:8, 21, 39; 4:5, 14, 26) and also in Joshua (Josh. 24:8). Thus, as in Jeremiah 49:2 (expected second conquest of Ammon in the last days), a second conquest motif (i.e., usage of Canaanites in Obad. 20) appears in Israel's possession of the hill country of Edom and territories of other enemies (vv. 17–20).

Contribution to the Bible

Like the book of Revelation which proclaims the downfall of the persecuting Roman Empire, the book of Obadiah sustains faith in God's moral government and hope in the eventual triumph of his just will. It brings a pastoral message to aching hearts that God is on his throne, and he cares for his own.

Structure

The text declares the book of Obadiah a prophetic "vision" from the Lord (v. 1) which appears to be a war oracle (v. 1) communicating Yahweh's imminent judgment upon Edom (vv. 2–9). As subtype of the prophetic oracle against the foreign nations (Isa. 13–23, Jer. 46–51, Ezek. 25–32, Amos 1–2, Zeph. 2:4–15), it is typically announcing judgment on a foreign power (specifically Edom; see also Lam. 4:21–22) to bring deliverance for Judah (Obad.

17–20; see Jer. 46:25–28, Nah. 1:1–15, Zeph. 3:14–20). Yet Nahum and Jonah are atypical in focusing solely on judgment for a foreign nation, rather than specifying judgment for Israel as well.

The shortest book consists of several parts. First is a war oracle from the Lord announcing certain judgment on Edom for their arrogant presumption and self-deception (v. 3) that they were immune from divine intervention (vv. 1–9). Next is an explanation of the further cause for the coming judgment on Edom (vv. 10–14)—a lack of brotherly commitment (vv. 10–11) in gloating over the day of disaster for God's people, Judah, (vv. 12–13) and cooperating with Judah's enemies in her destruction (vv. 10–11, 13–14). Then the text focuses on the Day of the Lord (vv. 15–21) in which imminent judgment on the historical nation of Edom (vv. 15–16), followed by the ultimate judgment on "Edom" as representative of Israel's end-time enemies (v. 16), would result in the deliverance of both Judah and Israel (vv. 17–21).

Outline

I. An Oracle of the Lord Against Edom (vv. 1–9)
II. Esau's sin against his brother Jacob (vv. 10–14)
III. The wider context—the Day of the Lord (vv. 15–18)
IV. House of Jacob will possess Edom's territory (vv. 1–21)

Jonah

Introduction

The book of Jonah, the fifth of the Minor Prophets, is more like the stories of the prophets found in the Historical books in both form and content. The book gives us a brief glimpse into the life of Jonah, the "wrong-way prophet" who ran from God and was swallowed by a fish. Throughout the book, we see evidence of God's grace and his love for all people.

Circumstances of writing

Author

The book is an anonymous narrative about Jonah.

Background

Jonah appears in 2 Kings 14:25 as a prophet from Gath-Hepher in the territory of Zebulon in Northern Israel. He was active around the first half of the eighth century BC. Jonah predicted the restoration of the northern kingdom's boundaries. This occurred during the reign of Jeroboam II (ca. 793–753 BC). This book about Jonah could have been composed at any time from the eighth century to the end of the OT period.

Jonah preached to the city of Nineveh. Nineveh was a major city of the Assyrians, a cruel and warlike people who were longtime enemies of Israel. Assyrian artwork emphasizes war, including scenes of execution, impalement, flaying the skin off prisoners, and beheadings. This explains Jonah's reluctance to preach to the infamous city of Nineveh.

The key debate about the book of Jonah is the question of its genre. Is Jonah history or parable? The parable view argues that Jonah is a fictional story or fable made up to convey a theological point about God's attitude toward Gentiles. Proponents of the parable view argue that the ironic fantastic events described by the book (e.g., Jonah living and praying in the stomach of a fish) is the author's way of tipping the reader off that this is not literal history. There are also historical difficulties that the fictional view would resolve: the exaggerated size of Nineveh (3:3) and the lack of extra-biblical Assyrian evidence to confirm that the city ever repented.

Five considerations suggest taking the book of Jonah as genuine history. First, Jonah was a real historical figure, said to be a prophet in 2 Kings 14:25. The book portrays Jonah as a flawed character. Were the book of Jonah a piece of fiction, it would be guilty of slander, saying something derogatory and untrue about a real person who is elsewhere presented positively.

Second, Jonah is part of the collection of twelve Minor Prophets. All the other books of this collection convey prophecies by genuine historical prophets. By placing Jonah in this collection, the compiler of the Minor Prophets signaled that he considered Jonah to be an historical account.

Third, the miracles in Jonah are not impossible for the God of the Bible. Presuming otherwise, some interpreters allow their antisupernaturalism to drive them to the parable view of Jonah.

Fourth, Jesus, in Matthew 12:39–41 and Luke 11:29–32, spoke of Jonah being in the fish and preaching in Nineveh as these were real events. In particular, Jesus's statement that "the men of Nineveh will stand up at the judgment with this generation and condemn it, because they repented at Jonah's proclamation" (Matt 12:41, Luke 11:32) make little sense if the people of Nineveh never actually repented due to Jonah's preaching. Unless one is willing to affirm that Jesus was wrong, it is best to say that the book of Jonah is historical

Finally, the historical difficulties in Jonah can largely be resolved (see note at 3:1–3).

Message and purpose

God's positive attitude toward Gentiles. In chapter 1, Gentile sailors learn to revere and worship Israel's God. Their reluctance to throw Jonah overboard shows that they were concerned to follow God's ethical demands by not taking innocent human life. In chapter 3, Nineveh's repentance shows that Gentiles can be saved too. God is interested in all people, a concern that anticipates the missionary mandate of the NT.

God's grace. "God was merciful and compassionate" (4:2) toward Nineveh, thus showing that the God of the OT is the God of grace.

God's sovereignty over nature. The book of Jonah portrays the sovereign power of God over the natural world. God can hurl and storm at people (1:4), raise up a plant miraculously as well as a worm to kill it (4:6–7), and use a great fish to swallow and save Jonah (1:17). All this shows God's control over nature.

The futility of running from God. The trouble that Jonah got into when he tried to run from God's calling is a warning to readers that running from God is futile and only invites unnecessary hardship.

Contribution to the Bible

The book of Jonah shows God's gracious concern for the whole world, his power over nature, and the futility of running from him. In addition, it foreshadows Jesus's burial and resurrection. Matthew 12:38–45 and Luke 11:24–32 compare the ministry of Jesus with that of Jonah, Jesus being the greater. Both texts see Jonah's great fish as a foreshadowing of Jesus's burial in the tomb, making Jonah a "type" of Christ. If Jonah actually died in the fish (see note at Jonah 2:2), then his resurrection further parallels the resurrection of Jesus.

Structure

The book of Jonah exhibits a high degree of Hebrew literary excellence. His style is rich and varied. It is considered by many as a masterpiece of rhetoric. There is symmetry and balance in the book, and it can be divided into two sections of two chapters each. The peak of the first discourse is marked by its poetic form, which has a higher prominence in narrative than prose. The peak in the second discourse is marked by the dialogue exchange between Jonah and God. The Lord and Jonah are indicated as the two main characters of the story by being the only ones who are named; the other characters are anonymous.

Phenomena of nature also serve in each half as props: wind, storm, sea, dry land, and fish in the first half; herd and flock, plant, worm, sun, and wind in the second half. When placed side by side, chapters 1 and 3 and chapters 2 and 4 can be seen as parallel. Finally, both chapters 1 and 3 begin with Jonah receiving a word from the Lord consisting of a call to go to Nineveh.

Outline

I. Jonah's flight from God (1:1–17)
   A. The Lord calls—Jonah rebels (1:1–3)
   B. The Lord sends a storm (1:4–6)
   C. The sailors intervene (1:7–16)
   D. The Lord sends a big fish (1:17)
II. Jonah's prayer of thanksgiving from the fish (2:1–10)
   A. Jonah prays (2:1–9)
   B. The Lord delivers Jonah (2:10)
III. Jonah's preaching in Nineveh (3:1–10)
   A. Jonah obeys the call (3:1–4)
   B. King and Ninevites repent (3:5–9)
   C. The Lord withholds judgment (3:10)
IV. Jonah's anger at God's mercy (4:1–11)
   A. The Lord displeases Jonah (4:1–5)
   B. Jonah displeases the Lord (4:4–10)
   C. The Lord shows great pity (4:11)

Micah

Introduction

Micah's name ("Who is like Yahweh?") found in the beginning of the book (1:1; an abbreviation of Micaiah, cp. Jer. 26:18) and the question Micah asked at the end of the book, "Who is God like you?" (Mic. 7:18), sum up the book's overall message: people should ponder the person, acts, and character of the incomparable, "the Lord of all the earth" (4:13). He is incomparable in his holiness, power, and love. All people answer to this sovereign God for their worship and the kind of lives they lead. The rebellious and sinful will meet his judgment (1:5), but those who earnestly watch and wait for him will find his listening ear (7:7).

Circumstances of writing

Author

Micah's hometown of Moresheth-gath (1:1, 14) in the lowland of Judah was about twenty-five miles southwest of Jerusalem. The fact that his hometown is mentioned probably means that Micah ministered elsewhere, including Jerusalem, and since no genealogy is given, we can assume that his family was not prominent. Though from the country, Micah was no bumpkin. He was a skilled orator, a master of metaphors, with genius for wordplay and blunt, vivid imagery. Few prophets saw the future more clearly. Micah prophesied the fall of Samaria (1:5–9), Jerusalem's destruction (1:1–16, 3:12), the Babylonian captivity and return from exile (4:6–10), as well as the birth of God's future Davidic ruler in Bethlehem (5:2).

Micah's ministry probably began late in Jotham's reign and ended early in Hezekiah's, dating between 730 and 690 BC. His reference to the future judgment of Samaria (1:6) shows that his ministry began sometime before 722 BC. As such, Micah's ministry overlapped Isaiah's. The elders in Jeremiah's day remembered Micah's prophecy as having spurred Hezekiah's religious reform (Jer. 26:17–19).

Background

Both Israel and Judah experienced affluence and material prosperity in the late eight century BC. In the south, King Uzziah's military victories brought wealth for some. A wealthy merchant class developed, and many poorer farmers found themselves at the mercy of government-supported businessmen. As business dealings became more corrupt, God's prophets spoke to the nation, confronting the ill-gotten wealth and accompanying godliness. Amos and Hosea prophesied in the northern kingdom of Israel, and Isaiah and Micah prophesied in Judah to the south.

Judah's commercial and secular culture replaced God's covenant ideal. The rich became wealthy at the expense of the poor. Micah saw this as an indication of a rotten social fabric and crumbling national foundation. God's people were to be different socially and economically. They were stewards of God's land (Lev. 25:23) that he had allotted to each family (Josh. 13–19). God's law protected family property rights (Lev. 25:1–55) and provided for the poor and less fortunate (Deut. 14:28–29, 15:7–11). But growing affluence in Micah's day led to increasing callousness toward the weak (Mic. 2:1–2) and blatant disregard for God's foundational laws (6:10–12). Judges and lawmakers became involved in conspiracy, bribery, and other corruption (3:1–3, 9–11).

Religious leaders were concerned more about making money than teaching God's words (3:11). The wealthy learned to separate their worship from everyday practice.

At this time, the ancient near East experienced an international power shift. Assyria was ascending, becoming one of the most evil, bloodthirsty, manipulative, and arrogant empires of the ancient world. Four Assyrian kings made military inroad into Palestine during Micah's ministry, taking Samaria in 722 BC and making Israel an Assyrian province. In 701 BC, Sennacherib took forty-six Judean towns and villages and besieged Jerusalem. King Hezekiah had allied with Egypt and Babylon against Assyria, for which both Micah and Isaiah urged him to repent. God miraculously spared Jerusalem (2 Kings 19:35–36, 2 Chron. 32:22–23; Isa. 37:36–37), and according to Micah, the Jerusalem siege was both an act of God's judgment and an occasion for God's deliverance.

Judah never learned its lesson. The people wavered between faith and apostasy and suffered many crises. Micah preached to people who had long since abandoned covenant loyalty, including the king, the royal court, judges, and religious leaders. As the rulers proved increasingly unfaithful, Micah prophesied Judah's destruction, an exile by the Babylonians in 586 BC. Beyond that, however, he saw a future restoration for a remnant of the people (539 BC).

Message and purpose

Micah sought "to proclaim to Jacob his rebellion and to Israel his sin" (3:8). He pronounced God's judgment to call his people to repentance. Injustice was rampant (2:1–2; 3:1–3, 9–11; 6:10–11), thus they would suffer destruction and exile (1:10–16), silence from God (3:6–7), and frustration (6:13–16). But Micah balanced his prophecy with hope of a remnant spared through God's judgment and glorious future restoration (2:12–13, 4:1–5, 5:5–9, 7:8–20).

Contribution to the Bible

Micah's holy and just God demands holiness and justice from all people. This is the "God" he requires (6:8). The people had grown content with going through religious motions while practicing very little genuine spiritual devotion. Even the religious leaders chose to speak popular messages in order to support their standard of living. Micah preached that true religion comes from a heart tuned to God, resulting in godly living. As such, religion and ethics are inseparable. People who refuse to repent will face his judgment, but the faithful will find his salvation and be led by God's King who would usher in his peace and prosperity.

Structure

Structured thematically as a balanced chiasm, the book highlights the central and final sections. Each matching section reflects on the other. This literary structure emphasizes Micah's main themes of Judah's social sins, the moral failure of its leadership, and the establishment of God's kingship over the land.

Outline

I. Coming defeat and destruction (1:1–16)
   A. God's condemnation of his people (1:1–7)
   B. Micah's lament (1:8–16)
II. Corruption of the people (2:1–13)
   A. Judgment on greedy oppressors (2:1–5)
   B. Rejection of God's word (2:6–11)
   C. Hope after judgment (2:12–13)
III. Corruption of the leaders (3:1–12)
   A. Unjust rulers and judges (3:1–4)
   B. False prophets and the true prophet (3:5–8)
   C. Corrupt leaders and Jerusalem's fall (3:9–12)
IV. Hope for glorious future restoration (4:1–5:15)
   A. The Lord rules over the nations (4:1–5)
   B. The remnant and the Lord's rule (4:6–10)
   C. The Lord's reversal of the present situation (4:11–5:1)
   D. The remnant and the Lord's ruler (5:2–9)
   E. The Lord rules over the nations (5:10–15)
V. Corruption of the city and its leaders (6:1–16)
   A. God's lawsuit against his people (6:1–8)

B. Accusation against Jerusalem (6:9–12)

C. God's verdict of judgment (6:13–16)

VI. Corruption of the people (7:1–7)

A. Lament over decadent society (7:1–6)

B. Waiting in hope (7:7)

VII. Future reversal of defeat and destruction (7:8–20)

A. God's anger over sin and his salvation (7:8–10)

B. An exodus from exile (7:11–17)

C. God's forgiveness of sin and his salvation (7:18–20)

Nahum

Introduction

The book of Nahum dramatically portrays God overwhelming Assyria to relieve his oppressed people. It was certainly a harsh message for Israel's enemies, but for the people of Judah, it was a message of hope.

Circumstances of writing

Author

The presumed author Nahum (1:1) is the only person with that name in the OT. Like Jonah in the previous century, Nahum prophesied judgment upon Nineveh. The Ninevites in Jonah's time had repented (Jon. 3). But now that Nineveh's leaders had resumed their wicked actions, the Lord called Nahum to reaffirm his coming judgment. Ironically, Nahum's Hebrew name means "comfort"—comfort for Judah (1:12–15) because its cruel overlord Assyria would be punished without any "comforters" (3:7). Except for the name of his hometown, Elkosh (1:1), nothing certain is known about Nahum.

Two events circumscribe the earliest and latest date for composition of the book of Nahum: the capture and downfall of Thebes in about 663 BC and announcements of Nineveh's certain destruction (1:1, 2:8, 3:7) which would happen in 612 BC. The book's emphasis on the fall of Thebes, seemingly a recent event, would favor a date shortly after 663 BC, during the reign of the notoriously wicked

King Manasseh (ca. 686–642 BC) and/or his evil son Amon (642–640 BC). Certainly, Nahum 1:12 (Assyria was still strong or at full strength and numerous) suggests a time before the decline of that empire. This fits the reign of cruel Ashurbanipal (ca. 668–627 BC) when Assyria was at the pinnacle of its power.

Background

The Assyrian capital Nineveh was located about 220 miles north of the modern Iraqi capital of Baghdad. In Nahum's time, Israel and Judah had experienced long and distressing affliction by the Assyrians. As early as Shalmaneser III (858–824 BC), King Jehu paid tribute to the Assyrians. The Lord often used Assyria as "the rod of my anger" (Isa. 10:5) to punish his people. Shalmaneser V (727–722 BC) and his successor Sargon II (722–705 BC) besieged and destroyed Samaria, taking the northern kingdom of Israel into captivity (2 Kings 17:3–6). Similarly, Sennacherib captured and devastated Judah, besieging Jerusalem by 701 BC (2 Kings 18–19, Isa. 36–37). During Ashurbanipal's reign (ca. 669–627 BC), Assyrian rulers were infamous for their cruelty (see notes at 3:10 and 3:19).

Message and purpose

Judgment. The main theme of the book is the impending judgment of Nineveh by the Lord (1:1, 8; 2:8–13; 3:7–19) by which he would deliver his people (1:12–15; cp. vv. 7–8). Yahweh would pay back Nineveh and the Assyrians in the same way they have mistreated their enemies. Since they were known for scattering their captives in brutal death marches, the Lord would send a scatterer (2:1) to disperse the Assyrians in retaliation for their cruelty (3:18–19; cp 3:10). Since Assyrians delighted in shedding blood and pilling up the corpses of their foes, he would transform Nineveh into a city of blood with piles of its own corpses (3:1–3).

As Assyrians had plucked the capital city Samaria like first ripe fig to devour her (fulfilling Isa. 28:4), so too the Lord would cause their capital Nineveh and other fortresses to fall into their enemies' hungry mouths (Nah. 3:12). Though Nineveh (like Thebes) was seemingly impregnable because of its military strength (3:8) and its allies (3:9), the Assyrians would be exiled as they had exiled the Egyptians (3:10).

God the caring Warrior. God's character portrayed as a powerful but caring warrior (1:2–7) was the propelling force behind Nineveh's judgment. The Lord's jealousy for his people and his wrath toward his enemies (1:2–3), balanced by his compassion and longsuffering nature (1:3, Exod. 34:6–7), seem to pivot on his great power (Nah. 1:3) and goodness (1:7). Yahweh the Warrior will take vengeance on his enemies (1:2, 3–6). The portrait of God's wrath is consistent with his promise to avenge the blood of his servants (Deut. 32:35–36, 42–43). Furthermore, God's goodness and compassion was not the doting love of a permissive or impotent grandparent (2 Pet. 3:9–10, 12). He was good or (kind) to those who took refuge in him (Nah. 1:7) while bringing destruction on his unrepentant enemies, including Nineveh (1:8).

Contribution to the Bible

The book of Nahum provides a great view of a powerful, just God who maintains his absolute moral standards and offers hope to those who are despised and downtrodden. Nahum teaches us to trust God. Even when we despair of any help, we can know that God will stand with those who belong to him.

Structure

Nahum interweaved typical prophetic strands as judgment songs against God's enemies (1:9–11, 14; cp 12:13, 3:5–7), a woe oracle or mock lament (3:1–7), salvation oracle for his people Judah (1:12–15), a victory hymn to Yahweh, the divine Warrior (1:2–8; cp Exod. 15, Ps. 98), and sarcastic "word vision" of imminent enemy invasion (Nah. 2:1–10; cp 3:2–3). He colored this literary tapestry with satirical "taunt songs," mocking Nineveh's soon-coming role reversal (2:11–12, 3:8–19; cp. 2:1–2, 3:4–5). He ridiculed Nineveh's practice of scattering of people to other nations by announcing that

God's scatterer (2:1–2, 3:18–19) would pay her back in like manner. He taunted that her lion's lair or military booty would soon be looted (2:11–13). He also mocked her as a witch prostitute condemned to appropriate punishment: nakedness exposed with shame (3:4–7).

Using psychological warfare (as the Assyrians had used against Judah), Nahum taunted Nineveh's dependence on allies and other supposed defenses (3:8–10; cp. Isa. 36:4–20). Esar-haddon, father of Ashurbanipal, had threatened King Manasseh of Judah in 672 BC with treaty curses from the gods if they rebelled. As G. Johnston has argued, Yahweh converted borrowed treaty terminology to reverse this curse on Judah. It would not be Judah but Assyria's military men who would become defenseless like women (Nah. 3:13). The Assyrians' ravaging of the land like a swarming army locusts (cp. Joel 1:4–12; 2:4–9) was evoked and modified in order to mock Nineveh's merchants and military personnel, comparing them as harmless locusts on the wall, easily frightened and scattered (Nah. 3:15–18). The incurable disease threatened from their gods would boomerang and inflict Assyria instead (3:19).

Yahweh, as caring Warrior who would bring vengeance on his enemies, especially Nineveh, in order to save Judah, forms the backbone not only of Nahum's purpose statement but also of the book's literary structure.

Outline

    I.   Prelude (1:1–10)
    II.   Nineveh's destruction as part of God's plan (1:11–15)
        A.   Deliverance of Judah (1:12, 13, 15)
        B.   Judgment against Assyria (1:11, 14)
   III. Nineveh's destruction to be complete (2:1–13)
        A.   Successful siege (2:1–9)
        B.   Despair of the people (2:10–13)
   IV. Nineveh's destruction the result of sin (3:1–18)
        A.   Inevitability of judgment (3:1–4)
        B.   National annihilation (3:5–18)
    V.   Postlude (3:19)

Habakkuk

Introduction

One of the Minor Prophets, the book of Habakkuk is unique in its style. Rather than speaking to the people on God's behalf, he spoke to God on behalf of the people. He struggled with how to understand God's actions in history, especially his use of an unrighteous nation as the instrument of his justice. God's answer to Habakkuk's objection was that "the righteous one will live by faith" (2:4).

Circumstances of writing

Author

Habakkuk is not mentioned anywhere else in the Bible. His name is thought to derive from the Hebrew word *chabaq*, which means "to embrace," but its form appears non-Hebraic. More likely, the name is related to *habaququ*, a word found in the related Semitic language of Akkadian. It denotes a species of garden plant or fruit tree.

Background

Habakkuk predicted the invasion of Judah by the Chaldeans (1:6). The term *Chaldean* (Hebrew, *Kasdim*, *Akk kaldu*) was originally used of an ethnic group that appeared in southern Babylonia in the ninth century BC. In the eighth century BC, Chaldeans began to rise to power in Babylon. Among the early Chaldean kings was Merodach-baladan II (2 Kings 20:12, Isa. 39:1) who, twice in the late eighth century, took (and lost) Babylon's throne. The Chaldean Nabopolassar (626–605 BC) began to dismantle the Assyrian Empire with help from the Medes and founded the Neo-Babylonian Empire. By the time of Habakkuk, *Chaldean* had come to be a synonym for Babylonian.

These world events came to affect Judah. Pharaoh Neco of Egypt passed through Palestine in an attempt to support the remnant of the Assyrians in Northern Syria against Babylon. The godly King Josiah confronted him at Megiddo but was killed by Neco in 609 BC. Judah then fell into Egypt's hands from 609–605 BC.

Judah's fortunes changed again when Nabopolassar's son Nebuchadnezzar II defeated Neco at the battle of Carchemis (May/June 605 BC) on the Euphrates River of Aleppo and succeeded his father on the throne of Babylon in September of that year. The Babylonian army pursued Neco back to Egypt. This led to Judah's falling under control of the Babylonians by 604 BC.

Habakkuk predicted the Chaldean's devastation of Judah (1:5–11), but that does not seem to have been fulfilled by the relatively bloodless Babylonian occupation in 604 BC. But when Jehoiakim, whom Neco had placed on Judah's throne in 609 BC, rebelled against Babylon in roughly 600 BC, Nebuchadnezzar eventually invaded the land and besieged Jerusalem from 598 to 597 BC. This led to Jehoiakim being deposed and killed in 598 BC and his son Jehoiachin going into Babylonian exile in 597 BC. The last king of Judah, Zedekiah, brought even more devastation upon Judah by rebelling against Babylon in 588 BC. When Judah fell to the Babylonians in August of either 587 or 586 BC, Nebuchadnezzar devastated Jerusalem and destroyed the temple. And yet as Habakkuk predicted (2:6–20), Babylon had its own day of reckoning in 539 BC when Cyrus of Persia conquered it.

These historical events help us to attach a date to the book of Habakkuk. He probably wrote his prophecy during the time of trouble after the death of Judah's King Josiah in 609 BC but before the devastations of Judah in 598/597 BC by the Chaldeans. That places the prophecy during the reign of Jehoiakim (ca. 609–599 BC), probably in the period of Egyptian domination before Babylon invaded Judah (609–605 BC).

Message and purpose

Like the book of Job, Habakkuk deals with the problem of understanding God's ways: Why does God allow injustice to prevail (1:3)? How can God use the more wicked Babylonians to punish the less wicked Judeans (1:13)? How long will God allow evildoers to dominate the world (1:17)?

God did not give clear answers to the questions Habakkuk raised. Instead, he called on the godly to have faith (2:4). When Habakkuk declared he would rejoice in God no matter what (3:17–19), he showed that he had accepted and appropriated this message to his own life.

God's sovereign greatness. Habakkuk shows God's greatness. He is eternally alive (1:12), unlike dead idols of wood or stone (2:18–19). His prophecies come true (2:3). He can raise up nations to accomplish his purposes (1:6), and he shakes the world through pestilence and war (3:2–15).

God's hidden justice. Habakkuk's God is holy (1:12). The prophet expected him to expose injustice (1:2–4, 13a), though sometimes it is hard to see God's justice working through the events of human history (1:13b). But though God may use the wicked acts of men for his good purposes and allow evil to prevail for a time, ultimately, the wicked will pay for their crimes (2:6–14), and God will come to save his people and crush the wicked (3:13–15).

Faith. The key verse of Habakkuk is 2:4b: "The righteous one will live by faith." Though we find it difficult to fathom the ways of God with man, we can learn, as Habakkuk did, to trust and exult in God's goodness despite our imperfect understanding (3:16–19).

Contribution to the Bible

The book of Habakkuk looks at an issue that often confronts people: trying to discern God's purposes in the midst of this world. There is a realization of God's will for this world. This truth is found throughout Scripture: God's promises to Abraham; God's desire for us to have abundant life; and God's will for a human community of joy, security, and righteousness. We ultimately triumph in the world and live abundantly only through faith. Habakkuk's message that the righteous will live by faith prepared the way for the greater understanding of this truth in the NT, which emphasizes salvation through faith in Christ (Rom. 1:17, Gal. 3:11; Heb. 10:38–39).

Structure

The first two chapters consist of a dialogue between the prophet and God. Habakkuk first complained of injustice in Judah (1:2–4). God responded by announcing that he was sending the Chaldeans to punish Judah (1:5–11). Habakkuk then complained about God's answer, arguing that it was unfair for God to use the more wicked Babylonians to punish the less wicked Judeans (1:12–2:1). God responded that the Babylonians were indeed arrogant would ultimately punish; nonetheless, God would use the Babylonians as he had determined (2:2–20). The final chapter consists of psalm in which Habakkuk reflected on this dialogue with God.

Outline

I.   Dialogue between God and Habakkuk (1:2–2:20)
  A.   Habakkuk's first complaint—injustice (1:1–4)
  B.   God's first response—Chaldeans will invade (1:5–11)
  C.   Habakkuk's second complaint—God seems unfair (1:12–2:1)
  D.   God's second response—have faith, justice will prevail (2:2–20)

II. Habakkuk's psalm (3:1–19)
  A. Habakkuk's fear (3:1)
  B. God's theophany (3:2–15)
  C. Habakkuk's faith (3:16–19)

Zephaniah

One of the Minor Prophets, Zephaniah focuses on the need to live in righteousness before God. Of all the prophets, Zephaniah probably gave the most forceful description of judgment, but he also lifted up the possibility of restoration for those who repented and turned to righteousness.

Circumstances of writing

Author

Zephaniah's lengthy genealogy (1:1, four generations back to Hezekiah) suggests he was royal lineage. Why list four generations (other prophets, at most, listed two generations; see Zech. 1:1) unless this final name was significant? Perhaps his father's name was Cushi. People tended to suspect that Zephaniah was a mixed ancestry, including Cushite bloodlines. In fact, Zephaniah twice mentions the Cushites/Cush ("Ethiopians") in his short prophecy (2:2, 3:10), possibly suggesting his Cushite roots.

Internal evidence indicates the book of Zephaniah was written sometime between 640 and 612 BC. Zephaniah 1:1 refers to King Josiah's reign (ca. 640–609 BC), and 2:13–15 prophesies Nineveh's fall. Since Nineveh fell in 612 BC, Zephaniah's prophecies would have been given prior to that time. Furthermore, existing idolatrous practices in Judah (1:4–6) imply Zephaniah's ministry began before Josiah's reforms in roughly 621 BC (2 Kings 23).

Background:

King Josiah's father, King Amon (1:1), was a wicked man, as was his father before him, King Manasseh (2 Kings 21:1–7, 11, 16, 20–22). This heritage of wickedness help explain the rampant idolatry in the land when Josiah inherited the throne in 640 BC. Josiah struggled to squelch idolatry in Judah (Zeph. 1:4–9). Together, pagan and orthodox priests led worship of Yahweh while also bowing before Baal, Molech, and other pagan gods (1:4–6). The public reading of the book of the law (ca. 621 BC) helped spawn the reforms of Josiah as people repented and tore down numerous altars (cp Jer. 11:13) and other idolatrous paraphernalia of Baal and Molech (2 Kings 23:1–14; cp Zeph. 1:3–4). This included abolishing the false priests (2 Kings 23:5).

Message and purpose

In view of the impending destruction of the "Day of the Lord" (1:7–18, 2:2–3), Zephaniah's primary purpose was to extend an urgent invitation. He urged the people of Judah to seek Yahweh alone in righteousness and humility (2:1–3). The immediate purpose was to warn idolatrous Judah of the Lord's imminent judgment (1:4–13). The ultimate purpose was to call out a remnant from all nations (Judah, 2:7–9; Israel, 3:12–13; all nations, 3:9–10) to trust in Yahweh because of the coming day of his judgment upon the earth (1:2–3, 17–18).

The Day of the Lord. In biblical times, capturing a city through siege warfare took months or even years; only a truly mighty warrior king (see Yahweh's titles, 3:15, 17) would claim to win a battle or even a war in a single day. The Day of the Lord was any time he "visited" earth, whether to punish his enemies (1:7–9, 12) or save his people (2:7; cp 3:17). This will result in the salvation of his people from immediate hardships in some cases (2:7, 9), but the ultimate Day of the Lord will come in the end times (3:11–20; cp Joel 3:14–21, Zech. 14:1–14).

The remnant. Zephaniah emphasized that God's seemingly all-inclusive judgment(1:2–3, 17–18; cp 3:6, Amos 9:1–4) was not inconsistent with preserving a few survivors called the "remnant" of his people (see note at Zeph. 2:9). Although God would destroy the wicked of Judah and their foreign neighbor (2:4–9), he promised to preserve a remnant—including even foreign peoples—to worship Yahweh (3:9; cp 2:11b).

God's titles. Yahweh is both God of Israel (2:9a) and Lord (lit. "Yahweh") of Hosts (2:9a–10), Sovereign Ruler over all armies of heaven and earth. Yahweh, King of Israel (3:15), is both "warrior" and "Yahweh your God" who saves his people (3:17; cp Exod. 15:2–3, 13–18). Second, "the Lord God" (Hebrew, *Adonai Yahweh*), universal Master of the earth, pours out his wrath and overflowing anger in the Day of the Lord (Zeph. 1:7, 14–18) upon both idolatrous and complacent worshipers (1:4–13). Also, "Lord of Hosts" focused on his punishment of nations that mistreated his people (2:8–10) and his "starving" of their false gods (2:11). Thus Yahweh's jealous anger is released (1:18; cp Deut. 4:23–27), not only against Judah (Zeph. 2:2–3) but upon all earthly kingdoms (3:8). Yahweh is a righteous God who executes justice (3:5) in the midst of rebellious Judah (3:1–4) by purging out haughty rebels(3:11). Yet because of his love (3:17), this warrior King (3:15, 17) will thwart enemy oppressors to remove deserved punishment from his remnant and save them from harm (3:15–17, 19).

Contribution to the Bible

The promise of a remnant illustrates God's amazing grace counterbalancing his jealous wrath and blazing fury against the wicked (Nah. 1:2–8). He would judge the proud nations (Zeph. 2:8–11, 13–15) and purged the haughty braggarts from his people (3:11) to preserve the humble. Thus Zephaniah invited everyone who humbly obeyed the Lord to seek him for possible deliverance (2:2–3). The NT highlights the wonderful truth that all of us can find salvation through faith in Christ. Paul underscored the idea of the Jewish remnant and reminded us that the remnant is "chosen by grace," not by works (Rom. 11:5–6).

Structure

"The word of the Lord (lit Yahweh)" (1:1a) and "Yahweh has spoken" (3:20b) frame the whole book of Zephaniah to emphasize crucial complementary messages: imminent universal judgment (1:1–3:8) but eventual blessing for the remnant (3:9–20). The chiastic first section, interlaced by the reinforcing refrain "this is the Lord's declaration" (see 1:2–3, 10a; 2:9a; 3:8a; cp 2:5, "word of the Lord"), highlights an all-inclusive judgment.

Zephaniah 3:8 is a transitional exhortation that looks both backward ("therefore" [v. 8a]) and forward (wait patiently for God to consummate judgment which will yield salvation for the remnant [vv. 9–13], introduced by the Hebrew *ki,* "for because" [vv. 9, 11]). To offer hope during judgment, in 3:8–13, we may synthesize two exhortations; 1:17, hush/wait for the day of the Lord's "cutting off" the wicked, and 2:1–3, pivotal invitation to seek him for possible salvation.

Outline

I. Prophecy of God's judgment (1:1–2)
   A. Identity of the prophet (1:1)
   B. Announcement of certain judgment (1:2–6)
   C. Announcement of the Day of the Lord (1:7–9)
   D. The Day of the Lord, a day of woe (1:10–13)
   E. Judgment will not be delayed (1:14–18)
   F. Exhortation to repentance (2:1–3)
II. God's judgment to the nations (2:4–3:8)
   A. Destruction of Philistia announced (2:4–7)
   B. Moab and Ammon to be destroyed (2:8–11)
   C. Universality of the judgment (2:12–15)
   D. The corrupt city of Jerusalem (3:1–8)

III. Promised blessings (3:9–20)
    A. Salvation and deliverance (3:9–13)
    B. Salvation demands praise (3:14–20)

Haggai

—— ✺ ——

Introduction

Haggai challenged the discouraged people of Jerusalem to examine the way they were living and to set new priorities that would please God. They must remember that God was with them; he controls their future and want them to be holy.

Circumstances of writing

Author

There is no statement that strictly identifies who wrote this book, but the words recorded are repeatedly connected to what God spoke to the Prophet Haggai (1:1, 3, 13; 2:1, 10, 14, 20).

Background

In 587 BC, Nebuchadnezzar came to Jerusalem for the third time, this time destroying the wall, the temple, and the city (2 Kings 25:8–21, Jer. 39–40). Most of the people were taken into Babylonian captivity for seventy years (Jer. 25:11–12; 29:10), although Jeremiah and a few survivors stayed in Jerusalem (Jer. 41–43). God predicted through Isaiah that the strong named Cyrus (Isa. 44:24–45:2) would defeat Babylon and her gods (Isa. 46–47). After the Persian King Cyrus defeated Babylon, he issued a decree in 538 BC that allowed the exiled nations in Babylon to return to their homelands (Ezra

1:1–4; Cyrus Cylinder). Sheshbazzar (Ezra 1:8–11) led about 43,000 Jewish pilgrims back to the state of Yehud (Judah) to rebuild the temple in Jerusalem (Ezra 2:64–65). In the seventh month, the governor Zerubbabel and the high priest Jeshua led the people in building an altar to worship God (Ezra 3:1–7), then in their second year, the people laid the foundation of the new temple (Ezra 3:8–10). But this effort was stopped for the next sixteen years because the Samaritan people who lived north of Jerusalem frustrated these rebuilding efforts, plus they hired lawyers to cause the Persian authorities to stop supporting the work on this temple (Ezra 4:1–5).This led to a period of great discouragement. Apathy set in because many of the hopes of the Jewish people were unfulfilled. The walls of the city were not repaired, the temple was not rebuilt, there was a famine in the land (Hag. 2:9–11), and the people were still under Persian control. They could do nothing without the approval of Tattenai, the governor of the "region west of the Euphrates river," and his officials (Ezra 5:3–5). There seemed to be no way to move forward and rebuild the temple.

After the death of Cyrus, his son Cambyses became king (530–522 BC). He marched through Judah and conquered most of Egypt, but in his home, he died (possibly an assassination). A high army official named Darius took control of the Persian army, marched back to Babylon, defeated a rebel force led by Gaumata, and became king in 522 BC. Darius put down several revolts and reformed the satrapy administrative system, with the result that by 520 BC, the Persian Empire was at peace.

In the second year of Darius (520 BC [Hag. 1:1, Ezra 4:24–520), when the conflict over political control of the empire was over, God directed Haggai to encourage the leaders in Jerusalem to rebuild the temple. When the governor Tattenai heard about this rebuilding, he questioned the plan's legitimacy and wrote to Darius to find out whether the government was sanctioning this project (Ezra 5:3–17). Darius approved the rebuilding campaign and even supported it through the royal treasury, as was confirmed by the discovery of Cyrus's original decree in a palace at Ecbatana (Ezra 6:1–12).

Consequently, the temple rebuilding was completed in four years (Ezra 6:15).

Message and purpose

Through his message, Haggai tried to persuade his audience to glorify God by rebuilding the temple. He argued that one should not (a) focus on one's own needs (1:4); (b) be discouraged because it was not as glorious as Solomon's (2:3); (c) be unclean and unholy (2:10–14); nor (d) feel useless and powerless (2:20–23).

Contribution to the Bible

Throughout the Bible, there is a call and a reminder to place God first. The period following the return from exile was no exception. Haggai's challenge was to the postexilic community of Jews living in Jerusalem, not to simply focus on their own creature comforts but to honor God. This commitment would be reflected in their own work on the temple. Haggai's call was later reflected in the word of Jesus, "Seek first the kingdom of God and His righteousness, and all these things will be provided for you" (Matt 6:33). Haggai's call for the people to get their priorities in order and place God first by rebuilding his temple was of great importance. For the people to return to this task was a sign of their priorities. It also showed that God was with the remnant and that his promises of restoration had begun to be fulfilled. Their obedience in this matter declared God's glory and thus brought him pleasure. It served to vindicate the Lord since the temple's destruction had disgraced the Lord's name. Finally, their obedience to Haggai's words served as a pledge of the new covenant of the messianic age. The restoration of the temple was a sign that God had not revoked his covenant with Levi or his covenant with David. He would provide cleansing and restoration through a glorious temple and a messianic ruler.

Structure

The book of Haggai contains four short confrontational order that identify ways the leaders and people in Jerusalem should change their theological thinking and behavior. There is a logical progression in the structure. People must glorify God (1:1–15), stay committed to God's plans (2:1–9), please God by living holy lives (2:10–19), and serve him faithfully (2:20–23).

Outline

    I.   Reprimand and call to rebuild the house of God (1:1–15)
    II.   Reminder of the Lord's presence and future glory of the temple (2:1–9)
    III. Religious principles about holiness and uncleanness (2:10–19)
    IV. Restoration of Davidic line promised (@:20–23).

Zechariah

Introduction

Zechariah prophesied to a group of discouraged Israelites, announcing that it was a new day for God's chosen people. He sought to inspire those who had returned from captivity to rebuild the temple and rededicate their lives to the Lord. The message of encouragement involved surrealistic visions and vivid poetic images, focused on a reversal of God's judgment, and called for a reversal of the people's behavior.

Circumstances of writing

Author

Zechariah returned to Judah with the former exiles and was apparently a priest (Neh. 12:16). He was a contemporary of Haggai. Though nothing is known of cooperation between the two prophets, they had similar missions and are credited with the successful reconstruction of the temple (Ezra 5:1–2, 6:14). Zechariah gave dates for two periods of his prophetic ministry (520 BC and 518 BC [Zech. 1:1, 7; 7:1]). Whether he is the author of the entire book is debatable. Many scholars, impressed with the differences between chapter 1–8 and 9–14, conclude that Zechariah did not write the last six chapters. It is not a major issue. The concept of authorship at the time of the Bible was different from modern standards. In the OT, there is evidence of portions of books under a single author's name that were not written by that author (Num. 12:3, Deut. 34:5–12, Jer. 51:64c).

Background

A key moment in the history of the Israelites came after King Cyrus of Persia granted the captives permission to return to Palestine (538 BC). The chosen people had just come through one of the worst experiences possible in the ancient world. Their homeland was devastated by invading armies, their capital city and temple were plundered and flattened, many of their people and leaders were killed, and most of the rest were carried off into pagan lands. The returnees who made the long trek back to Judah were faced with the challenge of reestablishing Jerusalem and the temple. Based on the account of the book of Ezra, work began immediately. But after the altar was rebuilt and the foundation stones were laid, problems arose, and the work stopped (3:1–4:24). Though sacrifices were offered on the altar, the temple continued to lie in ruins for almost two more decades.

Message and purpose

Covenant relationship. The message of Zechariah was both encouraging and challenging. With God empowering the chosen people, nothing would be impossible, not even rebuilding the temple. But Zechariah was concerned with more than bricks and mortar. The fundamental issue was the covenant between the Lord and the Israelites. God would not be satisfied with just a rebuilt temple and city. He wanted a restored relationship. Because their ancestors had failed miserably in obeying the law—not worshipping him in spirit and in the truth and by not acting justly toward one another—God called on the surrounding nations to punish his people. Now the question was whether the returnees had learned the hard lesson and would do any better at complying with the terms of the covenant.

Criticizing and energizing. Zechariah's message carried high stakes. The remnant that came out of the captivity was the only hope for the future of Israel. Based on the track record of the first generation, strong language would be necessary to penetrate the stubborn shoulders, closed ears, and rock-hard hearts of God's people (7:11–12). The method Zechariah adopted was to criticize the worldview that was dominant in the thinking of the Israelites and to energize them with the possibility of a completely new reality. Poetry served this purpose well because it allowed for language with the volume turned up.

Contribution to the Bible

The book of Zechariah is full of the language of judgment, but it is also full of God's promises. The Lord challenged his people to undertake overwhelmingly difficult tasks, and He assured them of their success through his power. But the nature of these promises extended beyond rebuilding the temple. From beginning to the end, the Bible tells the story of God's redemptive plan, culminating in God's triumph over evil and salvation for sinners. Zechariah's prophecies anticipate this grand culmination of history, describing a coming glorious king, a God who triumphs over all, and a world with all wrongs corrected. These promises set the stage for God's future kingdom as evidenced by the quotes and allusions to Zechariah in the NT.

Structure

The book of Zechariah is complex, sometimes with seemingly disjointed units, like a series of snapshots that need to be put in order. The apparent lack of organization may reflect the oral origin of the book, a collection of sermons that were patched together in written form. But it may also have been intentional. With the goal of shocking the hearers and bringing them to their senses, rapid-fire movement from one thought to another may have been part of Zechariah's technique. Chapters 1–8 contain carefully dated visions and sermons, while chapters 9–14 consist of undated poetic oracle and narrative descriptions of judgment and blessing.

Zechariah used a mix of genres.

His sermons, poetry, and oracle of judgment and salvation were typical of the prophetic genre. But his visions had similarities with apocalyptic literature, best represented in the OT by the book of Daniel. The content of some of his oracles, describing divine intervention and a radically different world, are also typical of apocalyptic literature. Thus, Zechariah may represent a stage of development between a prophetic form and an apocalyptic form.

Outline

I. Call to conversion (1:1–6)
II. Visionary disclosure of God's purposes (1:7–6:15)
    A. Vision one—appearances deceive (1:7–17)
    B. Vision two—the destroyers destroyed (1:18–21)
    C. Vision three—perfect safety of an open city (:1–13)
    D. Vision four—Satan silenced (3:1–10)
    E. Vision five—the temple rebuilt (4:1–14)
    F. Vision six—the curse destroyed sin (5:1–4)
    G. Vision seven—sin banished from the land (5:5–11)
    H. Vision eight-four chariots (6:1–8)
    I. Coronation scene (6:9–15)
III. A prophetic message to the people (7:1–8:23)
    A. Empty worship and judgment (7:1–14)
    B. Incredible blessings (8:1–23)
IV. The emerging kingdom (9:1–14:21)
    A. The king and his kingdom (9:1–11)
    A. Two shepherds (11:4–17)
    B. Inward blessings promised (12:10–14)
    C. Threefold purification (13:1–6)
    D. Death of the shepherd (13:7–9)
    E. The Day of the Lord (14:1–21)

Malachi

Introduction

Malachi is the last prophetic message from God before the close of the Old Testament period (although nonprophetic books such as Ezra-Nehemiah and Chronicles may have been written later). This small book captures the essential message of the Old Testament and shows the reader God's nature and our relationship and responsibility to him and to others in the covenant community.

Circumstances of writing

Author

Nothing is known about the author except his name. The book emphasizes the message rather than the messenger; God is the speaker in about forty-seven of the fifty-five verses. The one prophesized in 3:1 to "clear the way" for God to come to his temple is identified as (Hebrew) *malakiy*, "My messenger," a word identical to the name of the book's author.

Background

Although the book is not dated by a reference to a ruler or a specific event, internal evidence as well as its position in the canon favors a postexilic date. Reference to a governor in 1:8 favors the Persian period when Judah was a province or subprovince of the Persian satrapy Abar Nahara, which included Palestine, Syria, Phoenicia, Cyprus and, until 485 BC, Babylon. The temple had been rebuilt (515 BC) and worship reestablished there (1:6–11; 2:1–3; 3:1, 10). But the excitement and enthusiasm for which the Prophets Haggai and Zechariah were the catalysts has waned. The social and religious problems that Malachi addressed reflect the situation portrayed in Ezra 9 and 10 and Nehemiah 5 and 13, suggesting dates not long before Ezra's return to Judah (ca. 460 BC) or Nehemiah's second term as governor of Judah (Neh. 13:6–7; ca. 435 BC). Linguistic data favors the early date.

Message and purpose

Like Nahum (Nah. 1:1) and Habakkuk (Hab. 1:1), this book is called an "oracle" (Mal. 1:1). This Hebrew word *massa* is found twenty times in the OT (e.g., 2 Kings 9:25; Isa. 13:1; Ezra 9:1, 12:1). Once thought to mean "burden," it is now understood to refer to a divine pronouncement through God's prophet.

Indictment. Malachi presented Judah's sins largely by quoting their own words, repeating their own thoughts, and describing their own attitudes (1:2, 6–7, 12–13; 2:14,17; 3:7–8, 13–15). Malachi was faced with the failure of the priests to fear God and to serve the people continuously during difficult times. This had contributed to Judah's indifference toward God. Blaming their economic and social troubles on his supposed unfaithfulness, the people were treating one another faithlessly (especially their wives) and were profaning the temple by marrying pagan women. They were also withholding their tithes.

Instruction. God commanded sincere worship with genuine faith and humility. This included honoring him with pure offerings, being faithful to human covenants, especially marriage covenants, and renewing the tithe of all they acquired to signify their recognition of Yahweh as their God and King.

Judgment. If the priests would not change their behavior, God would curse them and remove them from service. Malachi also announced a coming day when the "God of justice" would come to judge the wicked and refine his people (Matt 3:12, 13:24–30).

Hope. As other incentives to obedience, Malachi pointed to (1) God's demonstration of love for Israel (1:2); (2) their spiritual and covenant unity with God and with one another (2:10); and (3) a coming day of salvation and blessing for those who fear him (3:1–6, 3:16–4).

Contribution to the Bible

Malachi was the last prophetic message from God before the close of the OT period. This book is a fitting conclusion of the OT and transition for understanding the kingdom proclamation in the NT. Malachi spoke to the hearts of a troubled people whose circumstances of financial insecurity, rebellious skepticism, and personal disappointments were similar to those often experienced by God's people today. The book contains a message that must not be overlooked by those who wish to encounter God and his kingdom and to lead others to a similar encounter. We have a great, loving, and holy God who has unchanging and glorious purposes for his people. Our God calls us to genuine worship, fidelity to himself and to one another, and to expectant faith in what he is doing and says he will do in this world and for his people.

God's love is paramount. It is expressed in Malachi in terms of God's election and protection of Israel above all nations of the world. Since God had served the interests of Judah out of his unchanging love, he required Judah to live up to its obligations by obedience, loyalty, and sincere worship. This love relationship between God and Judah is the model for how people were expected to treat other members of the redeemed community. They were required to be faithful in all their dealings with one another. As a community devoted to God, his people enjoy his protection and provision. But failure to live right before God and one another will bring God's judgment. Thus, God's people could not expect the joy of his blessings if they continued to fail in their duties to him and to one another. Before God would hold Judah in the balance of judgment, he would grant one last call for repentance. A forerunner would precede the fearsome Day of the Lord and herald the coming of God's kingdom on earth.

Structure

Malachi's message is communicated in three interrelated addresses. Each address contains five sections arranged in a mirrorlike repetitive structure surrounding a central section (a-b-c-b-a). The first two addresses begin with positive motivation or hope (1:2–5, 2:10a) and end with negative motivation or judgment (2:1–9, 3:1–6). In between is God's indictment (1:6–9 and 1:11–14; 2:10b–15a and 2:17) surrounding his commands (1:10, 2:15b–16). The final climactic address begins and ends with commands to repent (3:7–10a, 4:4–6). In between are sections of motivation (3:10b–12, 3:16–4:3) surrounding the indictment (3:13–15).

Outline

I.   Priests to honor Yahweh (1:1–2:9)
  A.   Positive motivation of the Lord's love (1:2–5)
  B.   Situation—failure to honor the Lord (1:6–9)
  C.   Command—stop the vain offerings (1:10)
  D.   Situation—priests profane the Lord's name (1:11–14)
  E.   Negative motivation—result of disobedience (2:1–9)
II. Judah exhorted the faithfulness (2:10–3:6)
  A.   Positive motivation—spiritual kinship among Israel (2:10a)
  B.   Situation—faithfulness against a covenant member (2:10b–15a)
  C.   Command—stop acting faithlessly (2:15b–16)
  D.   Situation—complaints of the Lord's injustice (2:17)
  E.   Negative motivation—coming messenger of judgment (3:1–6)
III. Judah exhorted to return to the Lord (3:7–4:6)
  A.   Command—return to the Lord with tithes (3:7–10a)
  B.   Positive motivation—future blessing (3:10b–12)

C. Situation—complacency in serving the Lord (3:13–15)
D. Motivation—the coming Day of the Lord (3:16–4:3)
E. Command—remember the law (4:4–6)

The New Testament

Matthew

Introduction

It seems fitting that the first book of the New Testament—the Gospel of Matthew—begins with these words: "The historical record of Jesus Christ." This Gospel was written from a strong Jewish perspective to show that Jesus truly is the Messiah promised in the Old Testament.

Circumstances of writing

Author

The author did not identify himself in the text. However, the title that ascribes this Gospel to Matthew appears in the earliest manuscripts and is possibly original. Titles became necessary to distinguish one Gospel from another when the four Gospels began to circulate as a single collection. Many early church fathers (Papias, Irenaeus, Pantanaeus, and Origen) acknowledged Matthew as the author. Papias also contended that Matthew first wrote in Hebrew, implying that this Gospel was later translated in Greek.

Many modern scholars dispute these traditional claims. For instance, against Papias, they argue that this Gospel was not originally written in Hebrew since the Greek of Matthew does not appear to be a translation to Greek. They further argue that if the early church, following Papias's opinion, was wrong about the original language, they were likely incorrect about the author as well. However, the excellent Greek of Matthew could have been produced by a skilled translator of an original Hebrew text. Furthermore, there are many hints of Hebraic influence in this Gospel (see notes at 1:17, 1:21, and 2:22–23). Finally, since Hebrew quickly ceased to be the dominant language of early Christians as the church expanded into Gentile territories, requiring the Gospel to circulate in a Greek translation, the absence of ancient Hebrew texts of Matthew is not surprising.

Even if Papias was wrong about the original language of the Gospel of Matthew, this does not imply that he and other church leaders were wrong to identify Matthew as the author of this Gospel. In fact, the early church unanimously affirmed that the Gospel of Matthew was authored by the Apostle Matthew. It would require impressive evidence to overturn this early consensus.

Clues from the Gospel itself support its ascription to Matthew. First, both Mark 2:14 and Luke 5:27 identify the tax collector whom Jesus called to be his disciple as Levi. This Gospel, however, identifies Levi as Matthew. Some believe Jesus gave the name *Matthew* (Hebrew for "gift of God") to Levi when he summoned him to be his disciple, but it was not uncommon for Jews at that time to have two names (like Saul and Paul).

The use of *Matthew* in this Gospel may be Matthew's personal touch, a self-reference that gives us a clue about authorship.

Background

Determining the date of composition of Matthew's Gospel depends largely on the relationship of the Gospel to one another. Most scholars believe that Matthew utilized Mark's Gospel in writing his own Gospel. If this is correct, Matthew's Gospel must postdate Mark's. However, the date of Mark's Gospel is also shrouded in mystery. Irenaeus (ca. AD 180) seems to claim that Mark wrote his Gospel after Peter's death in the mid-'60s. However, Clement of Alexandria, who wrote only twenty years after Irenaeus, claimed that Mark wrote his Gospel while Peter was still alive. Given the ambiguity of the historical evidence, a decision must be based on other factors.

The date of composition for Mark is best inferred from the date of Luke and Acts. The abrupt ending of Acts, which left Paul under house arrest in Rome, implied that Acts was written before Paul's release. Since one of the major themes of Acts is the legality of Christianity in the Roman Empire, one would have expected Luke to mention Paul's release by the emperor if it had already occurred.

This evidence dates Acts to the early 60s. Luke and Acts were two volumes of a single work as the prologue of these books demonstrate. Luke was written before Acts. Given the amount of research that Luke invested in the book and the travel that eyewitness interviews probably required, a date in the late '50s is reasonable. If Luke used Mark in writing his own Gospel, as seems likely, by implication, Mark was written sometime before late 50s, perhaps the early mid-50s. Thus, despite Matthew's dependence on Mark, Matthew may have been written any time beginning mid-50s once Mark was completed. The earliest historical evidence is consistent with this opinion, since Irenaeus (ca AD 180) claimed that Matthew wrote his Gospel while Peter and Paul were preaching in Rome (early 60s).

Message and purpose

Matthew probably wrote his Gospel in order to preserve written eyewitness testimony about the ministry of Jesus. Matthew's Gospel emphasizes certain theological truths. First, Jesus is the Messiah, the long-awaited King for God's people. Second, Jesus is the new Abraham, the founder of a new spiritual Israel consisting of all people who choose to follow him. This new Israel will consist of both Jews and Gentiles. Third, Jesus is the new Moses, the deliverer and instructor of God's people. Fourth, Jesus is the Emmanuel, the virgin-born son of God who fulfills the promises of the OT.

Contribution to the Bible

As the first book in the NT, the Gospel of Matthew serves as a gateway between the two testaments. Of the NT books, and certainly of the four Gospels, Matthew has the strongest connections to the

OT. Matthew gave us God's entire plan from Genesis to Revelation. Matthew looked back and referred to Hebrew prophecies about sixty times ("was fulfilled" and "so that what was spoken…might be fulfilled"). He also looked forward by dealing not only with Messiah's coming and his ministry but also his future plan for his church and kingdom.

Structure

Matthew divided his Gospel into three major sections. He introduced new major sections with the words "from then on Jesus began to" (4:17, 16:21). These traditional statements divide the Gospel into the introduction (1:1–4:16), body (4:17–16:20), and conclusion (16:21–28:20). Matthew also divided his Gospel into five major blocks of teaching, each of which concludes with a summary statement (8:1, 11:1, 13:53, 19:1, 26:1). Some scholars believe these five major discourses were meant to correspond to the five books of Moses and to confirm Jesus's identity as the new Moses.

Outline

I.   Birth and infancy of Jesus (1:1–2:23)
    A.   Genealogy (1:1–17)
    B.   Birth narratives (1:18–2:18)
    C.   Settlement in Nazareth (2:19–23)
II. Beginning of Jesus's ministry in Galilee (3:1–4:25)
    A.   Ministry of John the Baptist (3:1–12)
    B.   Baptism of Jesus (3:13–17)
    C.   Temptation of Jesus (4:1–11)
    D.   Summary of Galilean ministry (4:12–25)
III. Discourse One—the Sermon on the Mount (5:1–7:29)
    A.   The Beatitudes (5:1–16)
    B.   Character of kingdom righteousness (5:17–48)
    C.   Practice of kingdom righteousness (6:1–7:12)
    D.   Choice of the kingdom (7:13–27)
    E.   Manner of Jesus's teaching(7:28–29)

IV. Jesus's first miracles (8:1–9:38)
    A. A series of miracles (8:1–9:38)
    B. The kingdom and the old order (9:9–17)
    C. More miracles (9:18–38)
V. Discourse Two—ministry of Jesus's disciples (10:1–42)
    A. The preachers and their mission (10:1–15)
    B. The response to be expected (10:16–42)
VI. Responses to Jesus's ministry (11:1–12:50)
    A. The kingdom and John the Baptist (11:1–15)
    B. Challenge to the present generation (11:16–30)
    C. Opposition to the kingdom (12:1–45)
    D. Fellowship in the kingdom (12:46–50)
VII. Discourse Three—parables about the kingdom (13:1–58)
    A. Parable of the sower (13:1–9)
    B. The parable method explained (13:10–23)
    C. Other parables (13:24–52)
    D. Response to Jesus's parables (13:53–58)
VIII. Close of Jesus's ministry in Galilee (14:1–17:27)
    A. Crisis opposition (14:1–15:20)
    B. Withdrawal to the north (15:21–39)
    C. Further conflict (16:1–12)
    D. Crisis of faith (15:13–20)
    E. Preparation of Jesus's disciples for his death (16:21–17:27)
IX. Discourse Four—character of Jesus's disciples (18:1–35)
    A. Humility (18:1–20)
    B. Forgiveness (18:21–35)
X. Jesus's ministry on the way to Jerusalem (19:1–20:34)
    A. Teachings on the way to Jerusalem (19:1–20:28)
    B. Healing at Jericho (20:29–34)
XI. Jesus's ministry in Jerusalem (21:1–23:39)
    A. Events in Jerusalem (21:1–22)
    B. Controversies with the Jews (21:23–22:46)
    C. Denunciation of the scribes and Pharisees (23:1–39)

XII. Discourse Five—Olivet Discourse (24:1–25:46)
    A. Prophecy of the coming of the kingdom (24:1–36)
    B. Exhortations to readiness (24:37–25:30)
    C. Judgment of the nations (25:31–46)
XIII. Betrayal, crucifixion and burial (26:1–27:66)
    A. The plot to betray Jesus (26:1–16)
    B. The Last Supper (26:17–30)
    C. Events in Gethsemane (26:31–56)
    D. The trials (26:57–27:26)
    E. Crucifixion and burial (27:27–66)
XIV. Resurrection and commission (28:1–20)
    A. Women and the angel at the tomb (28:1–10)
    B. False witness of the guards (28:11–15)
    C. Jesus's Great Commission (28:16–20)

Mark

Introduction

Mark's Gospel emphasizes actions and deeds. Jesus is on the go—healing, casting out demons, performing miracles, hurrying from place to place, and teaching. In Mark, everything happens *immediately*. As soon as one episode ends, another begins. The rapid pace slows down when Jesus enters Jerusalem (11:1). Thereafter, events are marked by days, and his final day by hours.

Circumstances of writing

Author

The Gospel of Mark is anonymous. Eusebius, the early church historian, writing in AD 326, preserved the word of Papias, an early church father. Papias quoted "the elder," probably John, as saying that Mark recorded Peter's preaching about the things Jesus said and did but not in order. Thus, Mark was considered the author of this Gospel even in the first century.

The Mark who wrote this Gospel was John Mark, the son of a widow named Mary, in whose house the church in Jerusalem sometimes gathered (Acts 12:12–17) and where Jesus possibly ate the last supper with his disciples. Mark was Barnabas's cousin (Col. 4:10), and he accompanied Barnabas and Paul back to Antioch after their famine relief mission to Jerusalem (Acts 12:25). Mark next went with

Barnabas and Paul on part of the first missionary journey as an assistant (Act 13:5), but in Perga, Mark turned back (Acts 13:13).

When the Apostle Peter wrote to the churches in Asia Minor shortly before his martyrdom, he sent greetings from Mark, whom he called "my son" (1 Pet. 5:13). Then shortly before his execution, Paul asked Timothy to "bring Mark with you, for he is useful to me for the ministry" (2 Tim. 4:11). After Paul's execution, Mark is said to have moved to Egypt, established churches, and served them in Alexandria (Eusebius, *Ecclesiastical History*, 2:16). Some have suggested the young man in Mark 14:51–52 was Mark himself.

Background

According to the early church fathers, Mark wrote his Gospel in Rome just before or after Peter's martyrdom. Further confirmation of the Roman origin of Mark's Gospel is found in Mark 15:21 where Mark noted that Simon, a Cyrenian who carried Jesus's cross, was the father of Alexander and Rufus, men apparently known to the believers in Rome.

Because Mark wrote primarily for Roman Gentiles, he explained Jewish customs, translated Aramaic words and phrases into Greek, used Latin terms rather than their Greek equivalents, and rarely quote from the OT. Most Bible scholars are convinced that Mark was the earliest Gospel and served as one of the sources for Matthew and Luke.

Message and purpose

Mark's Gospel is a narrative about Jesus. Mark identified his theme in the first verse: "The Gospel of Jesus Christ, the Son of God." That Jesus is the divine Son of God is the major emphasis of his Gospel. God announced it at Jesus's baptism in 1:11. Demons and unclean spirits recognized and acknowledged it in 3:11 and 5:7. God reaffirmed it at the transfiguration in 9:7. Jesus taught it parabolically in 12:1–12, hinted at it in 13:32, and confessed it directly in 14:61–62. Finally, the Roman centurion confessed it openly and without qualification in 15:39. Thus, Mark's purpose was to summon people to repent and respond in faith to the good news of Jesus Christ, the Messiah, the Son of God (1:1, 15).

Contribution to the Bible

Many concepts of the Messiah existed in Jesus's day, and several individuals laid claim to the title. What Mark contributes is a clarification of the concept of Messiah and redefining the term. Peter's insightful confession at Caesarea Philippi in 8:29 became the turning point at which Jesus began to explain that the divine conception of the Messiah involved rejection, suffering, death, and resurrection (8:31). Mark also shows us the human side of Jesus. In fact, more than the other Gospel writers, Mark emphasizes Jesus's human side and his emotions. Thus, Mark gives us a strong picture of both the humanity and divinity of Jesus.

Structure

Mark's Gospel begins with a prologue (1:1–13), which is then followed by three major sections. The first (1:14–8:21) tells of Jesus's Galilean ministry. There Jesus healed and cast out demons and worked miracles. The second section (8:22–10:52) is transitional. Jesus began his journey that would take him to Jerusalem. The final section (11:1–16:8) involves a week in Jerusalem. From the time Jesus entered the city, he was at odds with the religious leaders who quickly brought about his execution. A brief appendix (16:9–20) in which some of Jesus's appearances, his commissioning of his disciples, and his ascension are recorded is attached to the Gospel.

Outline

    I.   Prologue to the Gospel (1:1–13)
    II.   Jesus's ministry in Galilee (1:14–8:21)
         A.   Events around Capernaum (1:14–45)
         B.   Five conflict stories (2:1–3:6)

    C. Jesus appoints twelve apostles (3:7–19)
    D. Charges about Jesus's mental state (3:20–30)
    E. Jesus's spiritual family (3:31–35)
    F. Jesus speaks in parables (4:1–34)
    G. Jesus's authority revealed (4:35–5:43)
    H. Rejection in Nazareth (6:1–6a)
    I. Jesus sends out his twelve disciples (6:6b–13)
    J. Death of John the Baptist (6:14–29)
    K. Jesus feeds 5,000 people (6:30–52)
    L. A third summary of Jesus's ministry (6:53–56)
    M. God's words or tradition of the elders (7:1–23)
    N. Ministry beyond Galilee (7:24–8:21)

III. On the way to Jerusalem (8:22–10:52)
    A. Blind man at Bethsaida (8:22–26)
    B. "You are the Messiah!" (8:27–9:1)
    C. Transformation on the mountain (9:2–13)
    D. The disciples' failure to cast out an evil spirit (9:14–29)
    E. Jesus's second prediction of his death (9:30–32)
    F. Who's the greatest? (9:33–50)
    G. Jesus teaches about divorce and remarriage (10:1–12)
    H. Jesus blesses little children (10:13–16)
    I. The rich man and possessions (10:17–31)
    J. Jesus's third prediction of his death (10:32–34)
    K. James and John make a request (10:35–45)
    L. Jesus heals the blind Bartimaeus (10:46–52)

IV. A week in Jerusalem (11:1–16:8)
    A. The royal procession (11:1–11)
    B. A barren tree and a barren temple (11:12–26)
    C. A series of conflict stories (11:27–12:44)
    D. Jesus predicts the temple's destruction (13:1–2)
    E. Jesus's Olivet Discourse (13:3–37)
    F. The Sanhedrin's plot to kill Jesus (14:1–2)
    G. Jesus anointed in Bethany (14:3–9)
    H. Judas makes a deal (14:10–11)
    I. The Passover meal (14:12–31)

Luke

Introduction

The Gospel of Luke is the longest book in the New Testament. Focusing on the life and ministry of Jesus Christ, this Gospel is part one of a two-part history, the book of Acts being part two. Both were dedicated to "most honorable Theophilus" (Luke 1:3, Acts 1:1).

Circumstances of writing

Author

The author of the third Gospel is not named. Considerable evidence points to Luke as the author. Much of that proof is found in the book of Acts which identifies itself as sequel to Luke (Acts 1:1–3). A major line of evidence has to do with the so-called "we" sections of the book (Acts 16:10–17, 20:5–15, 21:1–18, 27:1–37, 28:1–16). Most of Acts is narrated in third-person plural ("they," "them," but some later sections having to do with the ministry of the Apostle Paul unexpectedly shift to first-person plural—"we," "us"). This indicates that the author had joined the Apostle Paul for the events recorded in those passages. Since there are no "we" in the passages in the Gospel of Luke, that fits with the author stating that he used eyewitness testimony to the life of Jesus (1:2), indicating he was not such eyewitness himself. Among Paul's well-known coworkers, the most likely candidate is Luke, the doctor (see Col. 4:14, Philem. 24).

That is also the unanimous testimony of the earliest Christian writers (e.g., Justin Martyr, the Muratorian Canon, and Tertullian). Since Luke is not named among the workers who were "of the circumcision" (i.e., a Jew [Col. 4:11], he was almost certainly a Gentile. That explains the healthy emphasis on Gentiles in Luke [6:17, 7:1–10]). Luke also reflects an interest in medical matters (e.g., 4:38, 14:2).

Background

Traditionally, the Gospel of Luke is believed to have been written after both Matthew and Mark. Those who date Matthew and Mark in the '60s or '70s of the first century AD have tended to push the date of Luke back to '70s or '80s.

Since Luke wrote both the third Gospel and the book of Acts (Acts 1:1–3), it is relevant to consider the dating of both books together. The events at the end of Acts occurred around AD 62–63. That is the earliest point at which Acts could have been written. If Acts was written in the early 60s from Rome where Paul was imprisoned two years (Acts 28:30), the third Gospel could date from an earlier stage of that period of imprisonment. The other reasonable possibility is during Paul's earlier two years imprisonment in Caesarea (Acts 24:27). From that location, Luke would have been able to travel and interview the eyewitnesses to Jesus's life and ministry who were still alive.

The third Gospel is addressed to "most honorable Theophilus" (Luke 1:3), about whom nothing else is known other than that he is also the recipient of the book of Acts (1:1). The Greek name *Theophilus*, which means "lover of God or friend of God," implies that he was a Gentile, probably Greek. He seems to be a relatively new believer, recently instructed about Jesus and the Christian faith (Luke 1:4). The title "most honorable" indicates that at least, he was a person of high standing and financial substance. It may also reflect that he was an official with some governmental authority and power.

Message and purpose

The Gospel of Luke is a carefully researched (1:3) selective presentation of the person and life of Jesus Christ, designed to strengthen the faith of believers (1:3–4) and to challenge the misconceptions of unbelievers, especially those from a Greek background. Its portrait of Jesus is well-balanced, skillfully emphasizing his divinity and perfect humanity.

Contribution to the Bible

Nearly 60 percent of the material in the Gospel of Luke is unique. Thus, there is a great deal that readers of Scripture would not know if the third Gospel were not in the Bible. Notable among the larger distinctive portions are (1) much of the material in Luke 1–2 about the birth of John the Baptist and Jesus; (2) the only biblical material on Jesus's childhood and preministry adult life (2:40–52); (3) a genealogy for Jesus (3:23–38) that is significantly different from the one in Matthew 1:1–17; (4) most of the "travelogue" section about Jesus's journey to Jerusalem (Luke 9:51–19:44); (5) a considerably different slant on the destruction of the temple (21:5–38) from the Olivet Discourse in Matthew 24–25 and Mark 13; and (6) quite a bit of fresh material in the post-resurrection appearances, including the Emmaus Road, and distinctive statement of the Great Commission and the only description in the Gospel of Jesus's ascension into heaven (Luke 24:13–53).

Structure

Luke's distinctive "narrative about the events" (1:1) of Jesus's life is written in "orderly sequence" (1:3) though not in strict chronological sequence in many cases (as the note will explain at various points). Generally, after the key events leading up to the beginning of Christ's public ministry (1:5–4:13), the flow of the book is from his early ministry in and around Galilee (4:14–9:50), through an extended description of the ministry related to his journey in Jerusalem (:51–

19:44), climaxing in the events of Passion week and post-resurrection appearances in and around Jerusalem (19:45–24:53).

Outline

   I.   Preparation for Jesus's ministry (1:1–4:13)
- A. Formal prologue (1:1–4)
- B. Birth of John the Baptist and Jesus (1:5–2:20)
- C. Childhood and early adulthood of Jesus (2:21–52)
- D. Ministry of John the Baptist (3:1–22)
- E. Genealogy of Jesus (3:23–38)
- F. Testing of Jesus by the devil (4:1–13)

  II.   Jesus's ministry in Galilee (1:14–9:50)
- A. Early preaching in Galilee (4:14–44)
- B. Calling of disciples, then apostles (5:1–6:16)
- C. The sermon on the plain (6:17–49)
- D. Faith issues, the sending out of the twelve (7:1–9:17)
- E. Peter's confession and the transfiguration (9:18–50)

 III.   .Jesus's ministry in Judea and Perea (9:51–19:44)
- A. Setting out toward Jerusalem (9:51–13:21)
- B. Continuing toward Jerusalem (13:22–18:30)
- C. Final approach to Jerusalem (18:31–19:44)

 IV. Climax of Jesus's ministry in Jerusalem (19:45–24:53)
- A. Controversies and teaching (19:45–21:4)
- B. Prediction of the temple's destruction (21:5–38)
- C. Events of Jesus's final Passover (22:1–46)
- D. Betrayal, arrest, and trials (22:47–23:25)
- E. Crucifixion and burial (23:26–56)
- F. Resurrection, Great Commission, and ascension (24:1–53)

John

Introduction

The Gospel of John is different from the synoptic Gospels—Matthew, Mark, and Luke—in that over 90 percent of its material is unique. John's Gospel does not focus on the miracles, parables, and public speeches that are prominent in the other accounts. Instead, the Gospel of John emphasizes the identity of Jesus as the Son of God and how we, believers, should respond to his teachings.

Circumstances of writing

Author

A close reading of the Gospel of John suggests that the author was an apostle (1:14; cp. 2:11, 19:35), one of the twelve ("the disciple Jesus loved" [13:23, 19:26, 20:2, 21:20; cp. 21:24–25]), and still more specifically, John, the son of Zebedee (note the association of "the disciple Jesus loved" with Peter in 13:23–24; 18:15–16; 20:2–9; 21; in Luke 22:8; Acts 1:13, 3–4; 8:14–25; Gal. 2:9). The church fathers too attested to this identification (e.g., Irenaeus). Since the apostolic office was foundational in the history of the church (Acts 2:42, Eph. 2:20), the apostolic authorship of John's Gospel invests it with special authority as firsthand eyewitness (John 15:27, 1 John 1:1–4).

Background

The most plausible date of writing is the period between AD 70 (the date of the destruction of the temple) and 100 (the end of John's lifetime), with date in the 80s most likely. A date after 70 is suggested by the references to the sea of Tiberias in 6:1 and 21:1 (a name widely used for the Sea of Galilee only toward the end of the first century); Thomas's confession of Jesus as "my Lord and my God" in 20:28 (possibly by a statement against emperor worship in the time of Domitian); who sceased to be Jewish religious party after 70; and the comparative ease with which John equated Jesus with God (1:1, 14, 18; 10:30 ;20:28).

The testimony of the early church also favors a date after AD 70. Clement of Alexandria (cited in Eusebius, *Ecclesiastical History*, 6.14.7) stated, "Last of all, John, perceiving that the external facts had been made plain [in the other canonical Gospels]…composed a spiritual gospel." The most likely place of writing is Ephesus (Irenaeus, *Adversus haereses*, 3.1.2; cp. Eusebius, *Ecclesiastical History*, 3.1.1), one of the most important urban centers of the Roman Empire at the time, though the envisioned readership of John's Gospel transcends any one historical setting.

John's original audience was probably composed of people in the larger Greco-Roman world in Ephesus and beyond toward the close of the first century AD. Hence John frequently explained Jewish customs and Palestinian geography and translated Aramaic terms into Greek.

Message and purpose

The purpose statement in 20:30–31 indicates that John wrote with an evangelistic purpose, probably seeking to reach unbelievers through Christian readers of his Gospel. If the date of composition was after 70, the time of the destruction of the Jerusalem temple, it is likely that John sought to present Jesus as the new temple and center of worship for God's people in replacement of the old sanctuary.

The Deity of Jesus. John emphasized the Deity of Jesus from the beginning of his Gospel. The prologue affirms that he is the eternal Word (Greek, *logos*) who was with God and was God. Jesus used the significant phrase "I am" seven times in John, claiming the personal name of God as his own. In John, Jesus is always in charge and knows what will happen in advance.

Know and believe. Eternal life is knowing God and Jesus Christ (17:3). Further knowledge of God comes from believing and knowing Jesus. "Knowing" and "believing" are the key terms for John. Both occur over ninety times in this Gospel and are always used as verbs. Jesus's teaching in John reminds us that knowing God and believing in Jesus are expressed in action.

Contribution to the Bible

Of all the Gospels and any of the New Testament books, the Gospel of John most clearly teaches the Deity and preexistence of Christ (1:1–2, 18; 8:58; 17:5, 24; 20:28). Together with the Gospel of Matthew, it provides the most striking proofs of Jesus's messiahship. It does so by narrating seven messianic signs (see note at 2:11); by seven "I am" statements of Jesus (see note at 6:35, 48); by specific fulfillment quotations, especially at Jesus's Passion; and by showing how Jesus fulfilled the symbolism inherent in a variety of Jewish festivals and institutions. Jesus's messianic mission is shown to originate with God the Father, "The one who sent" Jesus (7:16, 18, 28, 33; 8:26, 29; 15:21), and to culminate in his commissioning of his new messianic community in the power of his Spirit (20:21–22). John's Trinitarian teaching is among the most overt presentation of the tri-unity of the Godhead—Father, Son, and Spirit—in the entire NT and has provided much of the material for early Trinitarian and Christological formulation in the history of the church.

Structure

John is divided into two main parts. In the first section (chs. 2–11), the focus is on both Jesus's ministry to "the world" and the signs he performs. Jesus performs seven signs that meet with varying responses. The second major section (chs. 12–21) reveals Jesus teaching to his disciples and the triumphant "hour" of his Passion. John's record of the Passion focuses on Jesus's control of the events. He had to instruct his adversaries on how to arrest him (18:4–8). Pilate struggled with his decision, but Jesus knew what would happen. Jesus died as the Lamb and was sacrificed at the very time lambs were being sacrificed for Passover (19:14).

Outline

I. Prologue—Christ as the eternal Word (1:1–18)
    A. The Word (1:1)
    B. The Word and creation (1:2–5)
    C. The Word and world (1:6–18)
II. Presentation of Christ as the Son of God (1:19–12:50)
    A. By John the Baptist (1:19–34)
    B. To his disciples (1:35–51)
    C. Through miraculous signs (2:1–12:50)
III. Instruction of the twelve by the Son of God (13:1–17:26)
    A. The Last Supper(13:1–38)
    B. The way to the Father (14:1–31)
    C. The true vine (15:1–27)
    D. The gift of the Spirit (16:33)
    E. Jesus's high priestly prayer (17:1–26)
IV. Suffering of Christ as the Son of God (18:1–20:31)
    A. His arrest, trial, and death (18:1–19:42)
    B. His triumph over death (20:1–31)
V. Epilogue—the continuing work of the Son of God (21:1–25)
    A. Appearances to his disciples (21:1–14)
    B. Assignment to his disciples (21:15–25)

Acts

Introduction

The book of Acts provides a glimpse of the first three decades of the early church (ca. AD 30–36) as it spread and multiplied after Jesus Christ's ascension. It is not a detailed comprehensive history. Rather, it focuses on the role played by Apostles Peter, who ministered to the Jews, and Paul, the apostle to the Gentiles.

Circumstances of writing

Author

The book of Acts is formally anonymous. The traditional view is that the author was the same person who wrote the Gospel of Luke—Luke, the physician and traveling companion of Paul (Col. 4:14, 2 Thess. 4:11, Philem. 24). As early as the second century AD, church leaders such as Irenaeus wrote that Luke was the author of Acts. Irenaeus based his view on the "we" passages in Acts, five sections where the author changed from the third person (*he*/*she* and *they*) to the first person plural (*we*) as he narrated the action (16:10–17, 20:5–15, 21:1–18, 27:1–29, 28:1–16). Irenaeus and many scholars since his time has interpreted these passages to mean that the author of Acts was an eyewitness companion of Paul. Luke fits this description better than any other candidate, especially given the similar themes between the Gospel of Luke and the book of Acts.

Background

The date of composition of the book of Acts is to a large extent directly tied to the issue of authorship. A number of scholars are argued that Acts should be dated to the early 60s (at the time of Paul's imprisonment). Acts close with Paul still in prison in Rome (28:30–31). Although it is possible that Luke wrote at a later date, a time when Paul has been released, it is more plausible to think that he completed this book while Paul was still in prison. Otherwise, he would have ended the book by telling about Paul's release.

Message and purpose

The book of Acts emphasizes God's work through the Holy Spirit in people's lives, those who devoted themselves to Jesus Christ, especially Paul as he led the Gentile missionary endeavor. It is no exaggeration to say that the Christian church was built through the dynamic power of the Spirit working through chosen vessels. Another important concept is the radial spread of the Gospel from Jesus to the Gentiles, from Jerusalem to Judea, from Samaria and to the rest of the world (1:8). Thus, Christianity transformed from being a sect within Judaism to a world religion that eventually gained welcome everywhere, even in the heart of pagan Roman Empire—Rome itself. At the heart of the Christian movement was the Apostle Paul's work, a former skeptic who became Christianity's most vocal advocate, from his first appearance at the stoning of Stephen (where he concurred in the decision to stone for Christian preaching), to his final appearance while imprisoned in his own rented house at Rome (where he was active in spreading the Gospel even when facing a death sentence). Paul's work on behalf of the Gospel is evident at almost every turn as he proclaimed the good news before "Gentiles, kings, and the Israelites" (9:15).

The book of Acts provides biographical glimpses of a few of the early apostles as they spread the Gospel first in Jerusalem and then on to the rest of the world.

Paul's typical missionary strategy was to go to a familiar place in each city he visited, usually a synagogue, and proclaim the Gospel first to local Jews. The speed with which he shifted his focus to Gentiles outside the synagogue edpede on how Jews received him within the synagogue. Before leaving town, Paul united Jewish and Gentile converts alike to form a local church.

The early apostles are distinguished by their being filled by the Holy Spirit and empowered to proclaim the Gospel under a variety of trying circumstances. The circumstances included theological, political, and physical oppression or a combination of these as they were marginalized, imprisoned, and stoned.

Nevertheless, through the power of the Holy Spirit, they refused to stop proclaiming the message that the OT prophesized about a coming Savior which was fulfilled in the person and work of Jesus Christ of Nazareth. As a result, many thousands of people in Jerusalem and abroad came to believe that the Lord Jesus is the Messiah, their one hope for salvation from their sins.

Contribution to the Bible

The book of Acts tied the other books of the NT together. It does so by first providing "the rest of the story" to the Gospels. The Gospel and the message of the kingdom did not end with Jesus's ascension to heaven forty days after his resurrection but continued in the lives of his followers. Acts shows us how the words and promises of Jesus were carried out by the apostles and other believers through the power of the Holy Spirit. Second, the book of Acts gives us the context for much of the rest of the NT, especially the Letters Paul wrote to the churches he had helped establish during his missionary journeys.

Structure

So far as literary form is concerned, the book of Acts is an ancient biography that focuses on several central characters, especially Peter and Paul. Ancient biography was not concerned simply with narrating events but with displaying the character of the people involved, especially their ethical behavior. Other features included genealogies and rhetorical elements such as speeches. Ancient biographies also commonly drew from both written and oral sources for information.

Acts 1:8 provides the introduction and outline for the book. Once empowered by the Holy Spirit, the disciples proclaimed the Gospel boldly in Jerusalem. As the book progresses, the Gospel spread further into Judea, Samaria, and finally into the outer reaches all over the world through the missionary work of Paul.

Outline

   I.   Empowerment for the church (1:1–2:47)
       A. Waiting for power (1:1–26)
       B. The source of power (2:1–13)
       C. Pentecostal witness to the dispersion (2:14–47)
  II.   Early days of the church (3:1–12:25)
       A. In Jerusalem (:1–7:60)
       B. In Samaria—the Samaritan Pentecost (8:1–25)
       C. To the ends of the earth—Phillip's witness (8:26–40)
       D. Conversion and preparation of Paul (9:1–31)
       E. In Judea—Peter in Caesarea (9:32–11:18)
       F. To the ends of the earth (11:19–12:25)
 III. Paul's first missionary journey (13:1–14:28)
       A. Cyprus (13:1–12)
       B. Pisidian Antioch (13:13–52)
       C. Iconium (14:1–7)
       D. Lystra, Derbe—return to Antioch (14:8–28)
 IV. The Jerusalem Council (16:1–35)
  V.   Paul's second missionary journey (15:36–18:22)
       A. Antioch to Troas (15:36–16:10)
       B. Troas to Athens (16:11–17:34)
       C. Corinth (18:1–22)
 VI. Paul's third missionary journey (18:23–21:16)
       A. The Ephesian Pentecost (18:23–19:41)

Romans

Introduction

Paul's Letter to the Roman house churches has been prominent among the NT writings for theological and pastoral influence. It focuses on the doctrine of salvation, including the practical implications for believers as they live out the salvation given to them through Jesus Christ.

Circumstances of writing

Author

Paul the apostle is the stated author of the book of Romans. From the book of Acts and the statements of Romans, we learn that Paul wrote this Letter while he was in Corinth and on his way to Jerusalem in the spring of AD 57 to deliver an offering from the Gentile churches to poor Jewish Christians (Acts 20:3; Rom. 15:25–29).

Background

All of Paul's writings grew out of his missionary/pastoral work and were about the problems and needs of local churches. The book of Romans is also of this genre, but it is the least "local" in the sense that Paul had not yet been to Rome. This Letter was his opportunity to expound the Good News message (the Gospel). He could discuss the essence of sin, the salvation accomplished on the cross, the union of the believer with Christ, how the Spirit works in the Christian to promote holiness, the place of the Jewish people in God's plan, future things, and Christian living or ethics. Though Paul did not write Romans as systematic theology, his somewhat orderly exposition has been the fountain for development of that discipline.

The origin of the Roman house churches is unknown. The founder of the Roman church likely goes back to the "visitors from Rome," "both Jews and proselytes," who came to Jerusalem at Pentecost (Acts 2:10). Many of these visitors converted to Christianity (Acts 2:41), some of whom very likely hailed from Rome. In Acts 18:2, Luke mentioned Aquila and Priscilla who left Rome because Emperor Claudius had ordered all Jews to leave the city (AD 49). This exodus was caused by strife among Jews over "Chrestus" (Christ). The remaining Christians in Rome would be from a Gentile background. The Jewish-Gentile tension in Rome had a long history. These tensions are somewhat reflected throughout the Letter, most specifically in chapters 2, 11, and 14 to 15. Rome was the primary destination of the Letter. Yet some manuscripts lack the phrase "in Rome" (1:7), giving some support to the conclusion that Paul intended a wider audience for the book of Romans and sent copies to other churches.

Message and purpose

Paul's purpose in writing Romans can be identified from his direct statements in the text and inferred from the content. He expressly wrote that he wanted to impart spiritual strength to the believers in Rome (1:11–12, 16:25–26). He asked for prayers for difficult tasks he was undertaking (15:32) and that he might be able to come and see them (15:30). He hoped to enlist the Roman churches to support a mission to the west (15:23–29). The content of the Letter shows that the churches experienced tensions between believers from different backgrounds. Paul wanted them to be united and to avoid dissension and false teaching (16:17–18). The content also reveals his exposition of what is essential Christianity and what are matters of indifference.

Contribution to the Bible

What is the Gospel? The word *gospel* means "good news." The good news is about Jesus and what he did for us. Most Bible students would say that the Gospel is outlined in 1 Corinthians 15:3–5. Romans fills in that outline and clarifies the Gospel in relation to the OT promises and the Mosaic law, the role of good work, and the gift of God's righteousness. Paul emphasized righteousness and justification in this Letter to a depth and detail not found elsewhere in the Bible. Sin is traced to its core in our union with Adam and the imputation of the original sin. Paul also mapped out the spread of human sin and its result in both believers and nonbelievers.

There are three passages in the NT (each one long sentence in the Greek text) that contain the most important theology of the NT: John 1:14 on the incarnation; Ephesians 1:3–14 about the triune purpose and God's glory; and Romans 3:21–26 on justification, redemption, and propitiation. If a Christian understands these three sentences, he has a solid foundation for faith.

Paul, in Romans 6–8, gave the most comprehensive development of our union with Christ and the Spirit's work in us. Romans 9–11 (on Israel's role in God's plan) has been called the key to understanding the Bible. Romans 13 is the classic NT passage on the Christian's relation to and duties to the state. Romans 14–15 covers how Christians can relate to one another, yet have different opinions and convictions on nonessential religious matters.

Structure

Paul wrote thirteen of the twenty-one Letters (or Epistles) contained in the NT. The four Gospels, the book of Acts, and the book of Revelation are not classified as Letters. Romans is the longest of Paul's Letters, and it contains the element found in a standard Letter at that time: salutation(1:1–7); thanksgiving (1:8–17); the main body (1:18–16:18); and a farewell (16:19–24). Some scholars refer to Romans as tractate (a formal treatise). But it bears all the marks of a real Letter, although it is a finely tuned literary composition.

Outline

1 Corinthians

Introduction

First Corinthians is the most literary of all Paul's Letters. With a variety of stylistic devices—irony, sarcasm, rhetorical questions, alliteration, antithesis, personification, framing devices, hyperbole, repetition, picturesque words (with local color), double meanings, and other wordplays—Paul *attempted* to persuade his readers. He wanted to communicate to the Corinthians the necessity of accepting the Lord's authority over their lives.

Circumstances of writing

Author

First Corinthians ascribes Paul as its author (1:1, 16:21). Biblical scholars are almost unanimous that Paul wrote the Letter. He wrote it during the last year of his three-year ministry at Ephesus, probably a few weeks before Pentecost in the spring of AD 56 (15:32, 16:8; Acts 20:31).

Background

During Paul's second missionary journey, he had a vision at Troas; he heard a man call him, "Cross over to Macedonia and help us" (Acts 16:9)! That change in plans led Paul to Philippi, Thessalonica, Athens and, ultimately, to Corinth (Acts 18:5). Paul ministered in

Corinth for at least eighteen months (Acts 18:1–18). He left Corinth accompanied by Aquila and Priscilla (Acts 18:18). Apollos then went to Corinth and had a powerful ministry there (Acts 18:27–19:1).

First Corinthians is the second Letter that Paul wrote to the Corinthian church. He had written them an earlier Letter that includes admonition not to mix with the sexually immoral (5:9). The writing of this second Letter (1 Corinthians) was completed by oral reports from Chloe's household about factional strife within the church (1:11). Paul had also received reports about an incestuous relationship among the membership (5:1), a faction that arose during observance of the Lord's supper (11:18), and confusion over the resurrection of the dead (15:12). As a result, Paul addressed these issues in 1 Corinthians. Apparently, as he was writing the Letter, he received a letter from the Corinthians asking his opinion on various issues (7:1, 25; 8:1; 12:1; 16:21). Therefore, he included his reply within this Letter to the Corinthian believers.

Message and purpose

In all of Paul's Letters, except Galatians, the main theme of the Letter can be identified by the content of the thanksgiving or by the stated reason for his giving thanks. The premise of each of his Letters also is usually found in the salutation beginning the Letter as well as in the introductory prayers following the thanksgiving section. Within his prescript and thanksgiving of 1 Corinthians, true to his custom, Paul presented the main theme of his Letter—that all believers belong to the Lord (1:2). Jesus is Lord; believers are his possession. For Paul, whatever issue was discussed, the answer of the issue was always addressed with the reminder of the Lord's authority over them (1:10). He used more than seventy-five idioms from first-century slavery to speak about the believer's relationship to the Lord, their master. Those who call upon the name of the Lord (1:2) are those who call upon his name as a sign of submission. In 1 Corinthians, "name" (1:2, 10, 13; 5:4; 6:11) is almost always synonymous with "authority."

Paul's purpose in writing 1 Corinthians was to motivate the Corinthian church to acknowledge the Lord's ownership of them and the implications this had in their lives. Key topics Paul addressed in this overarching theme of the ownership and authority of the Lord include Christian unity, morality, the role of the women, spiritual gift, and the resurrection.

Contribution to the Bible

First Corinthians contributes greatly to our understanding of the Christian life, ministry, and relationships by showing us how the members of the church—Christ's body—are to function together. Problems can arise in any church because the church is comprised of sinful people (redeemed, certainly, but still prone to follow the tug of sin). Paul gave specific solutions to specific problems, but the underlying answer to all these problems is for the church and its members to live Christ-centered lives. It comes down to living under the lordship and authority of Christ, the head of his body (the church).

Structure

Paul's writing is in the form of a Letter, using the standard four parts of a first-century Letter: salutations (1:1–3), thanksgiving (1:4–9), the main body (1:10–16:18), and a farewell (16:19–21). It is a pastoral Letter, driven by the occasion and the present needs of the recipients.

Perhaps the most noteworthy feature of the way Paul structured his Letter was his use of the word *about* to introduce a subject. It is apparent that "about" signals that Paul was responding to items on a list of questions that he had received—perhaps by way of a committee of men (16:17). These questions dealt with males and females in marriage (7:1); virgins (7:25); food offered to idols (8:1); spiritual gifts (12:1); the collection for the saints in Jerusalem (16:1); and Apollos (16:12).

Outline

I. Greetings and thanksgiving (1:1–9)
II. Problems in the church (1:10–6:20)
  A. Divisions and factions (1:10–4:21)
  B. Gross immorality (5:1–13)
  C. Litigation before pagan courts (6:1–11)
  D. Fornication with prostitutes (6:12–20)
III. Replies to questions from the Corinthians (7:1–14:40)
  A. Questions about marriage (7:1–40)
  B. Limitations of Christian liberty (8:1–11:1)
  C. Veiling of women in public worship (11:2–16)
  D. Disorderly behavior at the Lord's supper (11:17–34)
  E. Exercise of spiritual gifts (12:1–14:40)
IV. The resurrection of the body (15:1–58)
  A. Centrality of Christ's resurrection (15:1–20)
  B. Sequence of resurrection events (15:21–28)
  C. The resurrection and suffering (15:29–34)
  D. Nature of the resurrection body (15:35–49)
  E. The believer's victory over death (15:50–58)
V. Conclusion (16:1–24)
  A. Collection for the believers in Jerusalem (16:1–4)
  B. Paul's plans for visiting Corinth (16:5–9)
  C. Exhortations, instructions, and salutations (16:10–24)

2 Corinthians

Introduction

Of all Paul's Letters, none is more personally revealing of his heart than 2 Corinthians. At the same time, it is also the most defensive of any New Testament Letter. In it Paul mounts a strong argument ("apology" in the positive sense) for his authority and ministry. A number of important doctrines are taught in the Epistle, yet its greatest value may be that it reveals the heart and spirit of one of the most effective ministers of all time. We are thus shown that the genuine ministry—although it may have to be guarded from attack—is commissioned by Christ and empowered by the Spirit.

Circumstances of writing

Author

All biblical scholars agree that Paul wrote the Letter (1:1, 10:1). It contains more personal information about him than any other Letter, and its Greek style is especially like that of Romans and 1 Corinthians. Proposed chronologies of Paul's life and ministry include a number of variations. Yet for 2 Corinthians, the consensus is that the Letter was written about AD 56 (from Ephesus during Paul's third missionary journey).

Background

Although Bible students have often disagreed about the sequence of events that led to the writing of 2 Corinthians, the following scenario seems likely.

1. First Corinthians was not well received by the church of Corinth. Timothy had returned to Paul in Ephesus (1 Corinthians 4:17, 16:10). He reported that the church was still greatly troubled. This was partly caused by the arrival in Corinth of "false apostles" (2 Cor. 11:13–15). These were perhaps Judaizers, asking Corinthian believers of Gentile heritage to live according to Mosaic regulations (Gal. 2:14).

2. Paul visited Corinth a second time, the first time being his church-planting visit. He described this visit as sorrowful or painful (2:1, 13:2). Apparently, the false apostles agitated the Corinthians to disown Paul. This second visit, not mentioned in Acts 19, occurred sometime during the apostle's long ministry in Ephesus.

3. Paul then wrote a (now lost) severe letter of stinging rebuke to Corinth from Ephesus (2:3–4, 9). He sent this letter by Titus.

4. Titus came to Paul with the news that most of the Corinthian church had repented. They now accepted Paul's authority (7:5–7).

5. Paul decided to write to the Corinthians one more time, expressing his relief but still pleading with an unrepentant minority. He promised to come to Corinth a third time (12:14, 13:1). This was fulfilled when Paul stayed in Corinth while on his way to Jerusalem with the financial collection from many churches (Acts 20:2–3).

Message and purpose

Paul wrote to the Corinthian Christians mainly to express his joy that the majority had been restored to him, to ask for an offering on behalf of the poor saints in Jerusalem, and to defend his ministry as an apostle to the minority of unrepentant Corinthian believers. His desire was to encourage the majority and to lead the minority to change its mind about the validity of his apostolic ministry.

Important themes Paul developed in 2 Corinthians include the nature of apostolic authority and ministry, the new covenant, the intermediate state (the status of believers between the death of their bodies and the resurrection), and sacrificial giving. The overriding theme is the nature of true ministry. The diversity of these themes was driven by the circumstances that gave rise to the Epistle.

The matter of sacrificial giving is the focus of chapters 8–9, the most extensive NT teaching on Christian stewardship. Paul asked the churches he had founded to send generous offerings to the poor believers in Jerusalem. This occupied most of his energy during the last part of his third missionary journey. He mentioned it in his three longest Epistles (Rom. 15:28, 1 Cor. 16:1–4, 2 Cor. 8–9).

Contribution to the Bible

Second Corinthians contributes to our understanding of ministry. On this subject, we learn four key truths:

I. God was in Christ reconciling the world and himself and has given us a ministry of reconciliation.
2. True ministry in Christ's name involves both suffering and victory.
3. Serving Christ means ministering in his name to every need of the people.
4. Leaders in ministry need support and trust from those to whom they minister.

Structure

The Letter follows the standard format found in the other Letters bearing Paul's name. The salutation (1:1–2) and thanksgiving (1:3–11) at the beginning are followed by the main body of the Letter (1:12–13:10). A final greeting (13:11–13) stands as the conclusion.

The body of 2 Corinthians is the most disjointed of Paul's Letters. It is hard to miss Paul's change of tone from chapters 1–9 (which are warm and encouraging) to chapters 10–13 (which are harsh and threatening). Whatever one decides about the original unity of the Letter, no doubt the major turning point of 2 Corinthians occurs at 10:1.

Legally, because of the change of tone between the first part of the Letter and the last part, some interpreters had proposed a different understanding of the original form of 2 Corinthians. They proposed that two separate letters of Paul have been joined to make up what is now known as 2 Corinthians. What if, it was asked, chapters 10–13 were in fact the missing severe letter (2:4, 9) written after 1 Corinthians but before 2 Corinthians 1–9? The major differences in tone between these chapters would be more readily accounted for if this were true.

However, it seems much more plausible that the Letter originated in the form in which we now have it. All the ancient Christian writers knew the Letter only in its present form, which is to say unified as one single Letter. Surely within a single letter, an author may address two different sets of issues (a majority concern and a minority concern) and use two different tones (encouraging and threatening.)

Outline

    I.   Special greetings (1:1–11)
        A. Salutation (1:1–2)
        B. Expression of thanksgiving (1:3–11)
   II.   Clarification of Paul's ministry (1:12–7:16)
        A. Paul's itinerary explained (1:12–2:4)
        B. Forgiveness and recent travel (2:5–13)

Galatians

Introduction

Galatians, which may be the earliest of Paul's Letters, is also his most intense. It gives us a strong presentation of the truth that sinners are justified and lived godly lives by trusting in Jesus alone.

Circumstances of writing

Author

The author's name is "Paul," and he claims to be "an apostle" of Christ (Gal. 1:1). The autobiographical information in the Letter is consistent with what is known about the Apostle Paul from Acts and his other Letters. Everything in Galatians agrees with Paul's views elsewhere, notably in Romans.

Background

It is not certain where the Galatian churches were located or when Paul wrote Galatians. The reason is that during the NT era, the term *Galatians* was used both ethnically and politically. If *Galatians* is understood ethnically, the founding of the Galatian churches is only implied in NT. On Paul's second missionary journey, he "went through the region of Phrysia and Galatia" (Acts 16:6) in north Central Asia Minor (near the modern capital of Turkey—Ankara). His later visit to the same general area is recorded in Acts 18:23 and

19:1. This is where a group from Gaul (modern France) invaded in the third century BC, and it became known as Galatia.

Understood politically, Galatians can refer to those living in the southern part of the Roman province of Galatia. That region included the cities of Pisidian and Antioch, Iconium, Lystra, and Derbe where Paul worked to plant churches as recorded in Acts 13:14–14:23.

The view that Galatia was written to the area where the ethnic Galatians lived is called the North Galatian theory. The possible dates of writing related to this understanding range from AD 52 or 53, if shortly after the second missionary journey, to AD 56, if written about the same time as Romans to which it is similar theologically.

The view that Galatians was sent to churches in the southern portion of the Roman province of Galatia is known as Southern Galatian theory. Some holding this view date Galatians in the early 50s, but others as early as AD 48 or 49, before the Jerusalem Council, which is usually dated to AD 49. If the earlier date here is correct, Galatians is among the earliest of the NT books.

Another key consideration is comparing the basis of contention in Galatians in the topic of debate at the Jerusalem Council. The problem addressed in Galatians is that "the works of the law" of Moses (2:16–17, 3:2; cp 5:4), notably circumcision (5:2, 6:12–13), were added by some teachers to what was required in being justified before God. This is the same issue that Acts records as the reason why the Jerusalem Council met (Acts 15:1, 5), supporting the idea that the existing problem in the Galatian churches was part of the reason for the Jerusalem Council.

If Galatians was written after the Jerusalem Council, it is inconceivable that Paul would have cited the conclusions of the council which supported his works-free view of the Gospel. This strongly implies that the Jerusalem Council had not yet occurred when Paul wrote Galatians.

Message and purpose

Galatians was written and clarified and defended "the truth of the gospel" (2:5, 16) in the face of a false gospel. This was done by

(1) defending Paul's message and authority as an apostle, (2) considering the OT basis of the Gospel message, and (3) demonstrating how the Gospel message Paul preached worked practically in daily Christian living. Paul chose this approach to correct those in the Galatian churches in regard to both their faith and practice related to the Gospel.

Contribution to the Bible

There is much about the life and movements of the Apostle Paul that is only known—or filled in significantly—from Galatians 1:13–2:14 (and the personal glimpse in 4:13–14). Among these factors are Paul's sojourn in "Arabia" (1:17) and descriptions of two trips to Jerusalem (1:18–19, 2:1–10). Paul described a confrontation with Peter (2:11–14) that is mentioned nowhere else in the NT. In the middle third of Galatians, certain aspects of the Gospel's OT background are explained in unique ways. Notable are

1) the curse related to Jesus being crucified, as cited from Deuteronomy 21:23 (Gal. 3:13);
2) Jesus fulfilling the prophecy of the singular physical "seed" of Abraham (3:16; see Gen. 22:18);
3) the roles of the law as prison (3:22–23) and guardian (3:24–25) until Christ; and
4) the extended allegory of the slave and free sons of Abraham (4:21–31).

Galatians tells us much about the ministry of the Holy Spirit in relation to the Christian life. After the Spirit's role in the ministry of adoption (4:5–6), believers are commanded to "walk by the Spirit" (5:16), be "led by the Spirit" (5:18), and "follow the Spirit" (5:25), as well as "sow to the Spirit" and reap the related eternal harvest (6:8). The moment-by-moment outcome of that kind of sensitivity to the ministry of the Holy Spirit is what is meant by the "fruit of the Spirit" (5:22–23).

Outline

I. Introduction (1:1–9)
  A. Greeting (1:1–5)
  B. The Galatian's lapse from the Gospel (1:6–9)
II. The authenticity of Paul's message (1:10–2:21)
  A. Paul's Gospel revealed by Christ (1:10–24)
  B. Paul's Gospel acknowledged by others (2:1–10)
  C. Paul's Gospel versus Peter's compromise (2:11–21)
III. The way of salvation (3:1–4:31)
  A. Salvation is by faith, not by works (3:1–14)
  B. Salvation is through promise, not by law (3:15–22)
  C. Believers are sons, not slaves (3:23–4:31)
IV. The path of freedom (5:1–6:10)
  A. Freedom must not be lost through legalism (5:1–12)
  B. Freedom must not be abused through license (5:13–26)
  C. Freedom must be expressed through service (6:1–10)
V. Conclusion—sacrificial living versus legalism (6:11–18)

Philippians

Introduction

Philippians is Paul's most warmly personal Letter. After initial difficulties in the city of Philippi (Acts 16), a strong bond developed between Paul and the converts there. Paul wrote to thank the church for a gift it had recently sent him in prison and to inform them of his circumstances.

Circumstances of writing

Author

Paul the apostle wrote this short Letter, a fact that no scholar seriously questions.

Background

The traditional date for writing Philippians is during Paul's first Roman imprisonment (AD 62–62); few have challenged this conclusion.

Paul planted the church of Philippi during his second missionary journey (AD 51) in response to his "Macedonian vision" (Acts 16:9–19). This was the first church in Europe (Acts 16). The text of this Letter from Paul suggests several characteristics of the church at Philippi. First, Gentiles predominated. Few Jews lived in Philippi, and apparently, the church had few. Second, women had a significant role (Acts 16:11–15, Phil. 4:1–2). Third, the church was generous. Fourth, they remained deeply loyal to Paul.

Philippi, the ancient city of Krenides, had military significance. It was the capital of Alexander the Great, who renamed it for his father, Philip of Macedon, and it became the capital of the Greek Empire (332 BC). The Romans conquered Greece, and in the civil war after Julius Caesar's death (44 BC), Anthony and Octavius repopulated Philippi by allowing the defeated armies (Brutus and Cassius) to settle there (800 miles from Rome). They declared the city a Roman colony. It flourished, proud of its history and entrenched in Roman political and social life. In his Epistle to the Philippians, Paul alluded to military and political structures as metaphors for the church.

Paul wanted to thank the church for their financial support (4:10–20). He also addressed disunity and the threat of heresy. Disunity threatened the church, spawned by personal conflicts (4:2) and disagreement over theology (3:1–16). The heresy came from radical Jewish teachers. Paul addressed both issues personally and warmly.

The church at Philippi sent Epaphroditus to help Paul in Rome. While there, he became ill (2:25–28). The church learned of Epaphroditus's illness, and Paul wished to ease their concern for him. Some people possibly blamed Epaphroditus for failing his commission, but Paul commended him and sent home. Perhaps Epaphroditus carried this Letter with him.

Message and purpose

One purpose of this Letter was for Paul to explain his situation in Rome (1:12–26). Although he was concerned about the divided Christian community there, his outlook was strengthened by the knowledge that Christ was being magnified. Paul's theology of life formed the basis of his optimism. Whether he lived or died, whether he continued his service to others or went to be in Christ's presence, or whether he was appreciated or not, he wanted Christ to be glorified. Within his explanation are several messages.

Unity. Paul exhorted the church to unity (1:27–2:18). Two factors influenced him. The church in Rome was divided, and he lived with daily reminder of the defects of disunity. Further, similar disunity threatened the Philippian church as two prominent women differed with each other. Selfishness lay at the heart of the problems in Rome and Philippi. Paul reminded the believers of Jesus's humility. If they would allow the outlook of Christ to guide their lives, harmony would be restored. The hymn to Christ (2:5–11) dominate the Epistle.

Christian unity results when individuals develop the mind of Christ. In more difficult situations, the church collectively solved problems through the involvement of its leadership (4:2–3). Harmony, joy, and peace characterize the church that function as it should.

Freedom from legalism. Paul warned the church to beware of Jewish legalists (3:2-210). Legalistic Jewish teachers threatened to destroy the vitality of the congregation by calling to preoccupation with external religious matters. Paul countered the legalists with a forceful teaching about justification by faith. He chose to express his theology through his personal experience. He had lived their message and found it lacking.

Salvation. Salvation was provided by Christ who became obedient to death (2:6–8). It was proclaimed by a host of preachers who were anxious to advance the Gospel. It was promoted through varying circumstances of life—both good and bad—so that the lives of believers became powerful witnesses. Finally, salvation transforms Christians and churches into model spiritual life.

Stewardship. Paul thanked the Philippian believers for their financial support. The church had sent money and a trusted servant, Epaphroditus, to care for Paul. Their generosity encouraged Paul in time of personal need, and he took the opportunity to express the rewards of giving and to teach Christian living.

The church at Philippi had reached a majority regarding material possessions. It knew how to give out of poverty. It knew the value of supporting the Gospel and those who proclaim it, and it knew that God could provide for its needs as well. Paul also demonstrated his attitude toward material things. He could maintain spiritual equilibrium in the midst of fluctuating financial circumstances. Christ was his life, and Christ's provisions were all he needed. In everything, Paul's joy was that Christ was glorified in him.

Imitation. The Epistle abounds with Christian models for imitation. Most obviously, the church was to imitate Jesus, but other genuine Christians also merited appreciation. Paul, Timothy, and Epaphroditus embodied the selflessness that God desires in his people.

Contribution to the Bible

Paul's Letter to the Philippians teaches us much about genuine Christianity. While most of its themes may be found elsewhere in Scripture, it is within this Letter that we can see how those themes and messages impact life. Within the NT, Philippians contributes to our understanding of Christian commitment and what it means to be Christlike.

Structure

Philippians can be divided into four primary sections. Paul had definite concerns he wanted to express, and he also wrote to warn about false teachers who threatened the church. Many of Paul's Letters can be divided into theological and practical sections, but Philippians does not follow that pattern. Paul's theological instruction is woven throughout the fabric of a highly personal Letter.

Outline

    I.   Salutation (1:1–2)
   II.   Explanation of Paul's concerns (1:3–2:30)
       A. Paul's thanksgiving and prayer (1:3–11)
       B. Paul's joy in the progress of the Gospel (1:12–26)
       C. Exhortation to Christlike character (1:27–2:18)
       D. Paul's future plan (2:19–30)

III. Exhortations to Christian living (3:1–4:9)
    A. Exhortations to avoid false teachers (3:1–21)
    B. Miscellaneous exhortations (4:1–9)
IV. Expression of thanks and conclusion (4:10–24)
    A. Repeated thanks (4:10–20)
    B. Greetings and benediction (4:21–23)

Colossians

Introduction

Paul's Letter to the church at Colossae is one of the prison Letters (along with Ephesians, Philippians, and Philemon). Paul's desire with this Letter was to correct the false teachings that were cropping up in the church. In doing so, Paul presented a clear picture of Jesus Christ as supreme Lord of the universe, head of the church, and the only one through whom forgiveness is possible.

Circumstances of writing

Author

Colossians retains its place among the Epistles of Paul, who identified himself as the author (1:1, 4:18). The church fathers unreservedly endorsed Pauline authorship (Irenaeus, *Adversus haereses.*, 3.14.1; Tertullian, *De praescr. haer.*, 7; Clement of Alexandria, *Strom.*, 1.1; cp Justin, *Dialogue*, 85.2;138.2). A close reading of Colossians reveals a considerable number of lexical, grammatical, and theological similarities with the other Pauline writings (1:9, 26; 2:11–14, 16, 20–21; 3:1, 3, 5–17). Also favoring the authenticity of Colossians as a Letter of Paul is its close connection with Philemon, an Epistle widely regarded as Pauline.

Background

During his ministry in Ephesus (Acts 19:10), Paul sent Epaphras to spread the Gospel in the Lycus Valley. Epaphras subsequently established the church at Colossae (1:7, 4:12–13). The city's population consisted mostly of Phrygians and Greeks, but it also included a significant number of Jews. The church likewise was mostly composed of Gentiles (1:21, 27; 2:13), but it also had Jewish members (2:11, 16, 18, 21; 3:11). When Epaphras (Philem. 23) informed Paul of certain heretical teachings that had spread there, Paul wrote the Letter to the Colossians as theological antidote.

Paul wrote Colossians during his first Roman imprisonment (4:3, 10, 18; cp. Acts 28:30–31; Eusebius, *Ecclesiastical History*, 2.22.1) in the early AD 60s. Together with Philemon, Philippians, and Ephesians, Colossians is commonly classified as a prison Epistle. All four Epistles share several personal links that warrant this conclusion (Col. 1:7, 4:7–8, 17; Eph. 6:21–22; Philem. 2, 12, 23).

Message and purpose

Paul wrote to counter the "Colossian heresy" that he considered an affront to the Gospel of Jesus Christ. The false teaching is identified as a "philosophy" (2:8), presumably drawn from some Hellenistic tradition as indicated by the references to the "fullness" (1:19); the "elemental forces" (Greek, *stoicheia* [2:8, 20]); "wisdom" (2:3, 23); and "ascetic practices" (2:23). In addition, the false teaching contained Jewish elements such as circumcision (2:11, 3:11); "human tradition" (2:8); Sabbath observance, food regulation, festival participation (2:16); "the worship of angels" together with "access to a visionary realm" (2:18); and harsh human regulations (2:21–23). Paul addressed this syncretistic philosophy by setting forth a proper understanding of the Gospel of Jesus Christ and by noting appropriate implications for Christian conduct.

The heresy is not identified, but several characteristics of the heresy are discernible:

1) An inferior view of Christ is combated in 1:15–20. This Christological passage implies that the heretics did not consider Jesus to be fully divine or perhaps did not accept him as the sole source of redemption.

2) The Colossians were warned to beware of "philosophies" not built of Christ (2:8).

3) The heresy apparently involved the legalistic observance of "tradition," circumcision, and various dietary and festival laws (2:8, 11, 16, 21; 3:11).

4) The worship of angels and lesser spirits were encouraged by the false teachers (2:8, 18).

5) Asceticism, the deprivation or hash treatment of one's "evil" fleshly body, was promoted (2:20—23).

6) Finally, the false teachers claimed to have special insight (perhaps special revelations) which made them (rather than the apostles or the Scriptures) the ultimate source of truth (2:18–19).

Scholars cannot agree on who these false teachers were. Some of the characteristics cited above seem to be Jewish; others sound like Gnostic teachings. Some see the teachings of a Greek mystery religion here.

Theology of chapters 1 and 2 is followed by exhortations to live a Christian life in chapters 3 and 4. The commands "to put death" (3:5) and "now you must also put away" (3:8) the thing which will reap the wrath of God (3:5–11) are balanced by the command to "put on" (3:12) those things characteristic of God's chosen people (3:12–17). The changes are far from superficial, however. They stem from the Christian's new nature and submission to the rule of Christ in every area of life (3:9, 10, 15–17).

Rules for the household appear in 3:18–4:1. The typical first-century household is assumed; thus the passage addresses wives and husbands, fathers and children, masters and slaves. Paul made no comment about rightness or wrongness of the social structures; he accepted them as givens. Paul's concern was that the structures as they existed should be governed by Christian principles. Submission to the Lord (3:18, 20, 22; 4:1), Christian love (3:19), and the prospect of divine judgment (3:24–4:1) must determine the way people treat one another regardless of their social status. It is this Christian motivation which distinguishes these house rules from those featured in Jewish and pagan sources.

Contribution to the Bible

Colossians provides one of the Bible's fullest expressions of the Deity and supremacy of Christ. This is most evident in the magnificent hymn of praise (1:15–20) that sets forth Christ as the image of the invisible God, the creator and sustainer of the universe, and the head of his body, the church. In Christ are the "treasure of wisdom and knowledge" (2:3); because of him, "the entire fullness of God's nature dwells bodily" (2:9). The supremacy of Christ also has implication for the believer's salvation (2:10, 13, 20; 3:1, 11–12, 17) and conduct (3:5–4:6). Colossians contributes to Scripture a high Christology and a presentation of its implications for the believer's conduct.

Structure

Colossians may be divided onto two main parts. The first (1:3–2:23) is a polemic against false teachings. The second (3:1–4:17) is made up of exhortations to proper Christian living. This is typical of Paul's approach, presenting a theology position first, a position on which the practical exhortations are built. The introduction (1:1–2) is in the form of Hellenistic personal letter.

Notable in the final section is the mention of Onesimus (4:9), which links this Letter with Philemon, the mention of a letter at Laodicea (4:16) that may have been Ephesians, and Paul's concluding signature which indicates that the Letter was prepared by an amanuensis (secretary, see 4:18).

Outline

I.   Greeting and thanksgiving (1:1–12)
II. God's work in Christ (1:13–23)
    A. Redemption (1:13–14)
    B. The excellence of Christ (1:15–19)
    C. Reconciliation (1:20–23)
III. Paul's ministry (1:24–2:3)
    A. Minister of God's mystery (1:24–29)
    B. Sufferer for the Lord (2:1–3)
IV. False teaching denounced (2:4–23)
    A. Walking in Christ (2:4–7)
    B. Completeness of Christ's work (2:8–15)
    C. Exhortation against meaningless ritual (1:16–23)
V.   The Christian life (3:1–4:6)
    A. The new and the old (3:1–11)
    B. Exercise of Christian virtues (3:12–17)
    C. Family and social relationships (3:18–4:1)
    D. Exhortation to prayer (4:2–6)
VI. Conclusion (4:7–18)
    A. The mission of Tychicus (4:7–9)
    B. Greetings (4:10–18)

1 Thessalonians

Introduction

Paul spent a very short time in the city of Thessalonica, but he was able to establish a church during his stay. There may have been little time for instruction of the new converts, so it is not surprising that Paul wrote a letter to address some questions.

Circumstances of writing

Author

No serious objections have been made to dispute that Paul was the author of 1 Thessalonians (1:1). The greeting also mentions Silvanus and Timothy. Sometimes Paul wrote from the team perspective, but he was the primary author (2:18, 3:2).

Background

About AD 50, the missionary team led by Paul and Silas left Philippi and traveled westward on the Roman road known as the Via Egnatia. They proceeded toward the strategic capital city of the Roman province of Macedonia—Thessalonica.

Thessalonica was a large port city of the Aegean Sea in modern-day Greece, with a population of about two hundred thousand. The city was filled with pagan worshipers of idols, the full Pantheon of Greek and Roman gods, and was well-known for its emperor worship. Thessalonica was loyal to Caesar, and he had granted its citizens many privileges.

As was his custom, Paul found the local Jewish synagogue and started teaching there. For three Sabbaths, he reasoned with the Jews from the Scriptures. He explained and demonstrated that the promised Messiah had to suffer and rise from the dead. After explaining the life, death, and the resurrection of Jesus, he then stated boldly, "This Jesus I am proclaiming to you is the Messiah" (Acts 17:3). Some of the Jews were persuaded, along with some of the devout Greeks who were worshipers at the synagogue and some of the prominent women. They joined Paul and Silas, and the church in Thessalonica was born.

There were Jews in the city who were not persuaded, and they became jealous of what Paul and Silas had done.

They incited the people into an uproar and attacked Jason's house where the missionary team had been staying. They wanted to drag Paul and Silas out before the crowd; they found only Jason and some new believers. They dragged them out before the city authorities. The rulers, not wanting more unrest, forced Jason and the rest of the brothers to make a financial payment of security to ensure that there would not be a repeat of such a disturbance. That very night, Thessalonian believers sent Paul and Silas away to Berea where they could continue their ministry (Acts 17:1–9).

From Berea, Paul went to Athens. He wanted to see the Thessalonians again. When he could endure the separation no longer, he sent Timothy to encourage the Thessalonian believers (3:2). Timothy came back with an encouraging report about the Thessalonian church (3:6). Paul wrote to them from Corinth in response to Timothy's report. Based on archaeological evidence of a dated inscription mentioning Gallio, proconsul of Achaia, by name (Acts 18:12) and correlating this with Paul's visit to Corinth when Gallio was there, 1 Thessalonians is the earliest of Paul's Letters, with the probable exception of the book of Galatians.

Message and purpose

Timothy reported to Paul that although the church at Thessalonica was suffering affliction, they were holding fast to the faith. And though they had some doctrinal misunderstandings, they were laboring for the Lord out of love, and patiently for, the return of Christ. Paul wrote to encourage the church in their faith, to remind them that sanctification was God's will for them, and to correct misunderstandings about end-time events.

First Thessalonians presents four major themes.

Paul's conduct of his ministry. Paul's ministry centered on two aspects—the impartation of the word of God and the sharing of his life (2:8). The Gospel did not come in word only but in power and deed as well. Paul's motives were to please God (2:4, 4:1) and to express the concern for the Thessalonians' welfare (2:8). His message did not come in error, uncleanness, and deceit but in purity and truth (2:3, 10). Also, Paul didn't use his ministry as a cloak for covetousness (2:5). This was demonstrated by his working to provide for his material needs (2:9).

Persecution. The Thessalonian church was founded in the midst of persecution. Paul had to leave the city for that reason, and the church continued after he left (1:6, 2:14–15). Paul encouraged the believers there not to be shaken by these afflictions because Christians are certain to suffer (3:3–4).

Sanctification. Salvation is not finished once a person believes in Christ and receives forgiveness of sins. Paul's prayer for the believers at Thessalonica in 3:13 was that God would establish their hearts blameless in holiness before God. He pointed out that God's will for them was to abstain from sexual immorality and to love one another (4:1–12). Paul used his example of work to encourage them in their own work so they would not be unnecessarily dependent on anyone (4:10–12, 5:14).

Second coming of Christ. Jesus's return is mentioned in every chapter of 1 Thessalonians. Specific attitudes, events, and encouragements about "the Day of the Lord" are given with assurance that Christians are not appointed to God's wrath (5:9).

Contribution to the Bible

First Thessalonians contributes to our understanding of the second coming of Christ. Paul wrote to correct some misunderstandings of this doctrine, and in the process, he showed us that Christ's return gives us true hope. First Thessalonians and First Corinthians (ch. 15) are the only books that explicitly mention that Christians who are alive at Christ's return will be changed and will meet Christ in the air without dying.

Structure

First Thessalonians follows the standard form of first-century Letters: greeting (1:1), thanksgiving (1:2–4), body (1:5–5:22), and farewell (5:23–28). The body of the Letter does not follow Paul's typical structure of presenting doctrine first, followed by practical exhortation based on that doctrine. Instead, 1 Thessalonians moves back and forth between the doctrinal and the practical.

Outline

    I.   Greeting (1:1)
    II.   Commendation for the Thessalonians (1:2–10)
        A. Their work in the Gospel (1:2–4)
        B. Their reception of the Gospel (1:5–10)
   III. Conduct in ministry (2:1–16)
        A. Missionaries' visit example (2:1–12)
        B. Mixed responses to God's message (2:13–16)
   IV. Concern for the Thessalonians (2:17–3:13)
   V.   Call to sanctification (4:1–12)
        A. Abstain from sexual immorality (4:1–8)
        B. Practice brotherly love (4:9–12)
   VI. Christ's second coming (4:13–5:11)
        A. The rapture of the saints (4:13–18)
        B. The Day of the Lord (5:1–11)
   VII. Concluding exhortations and blessings (5:12–28)

2 Thessalonians

Introduction

Following up on the First Letter to the Thessalonians, Paul wrote to give further clarification on how to live the Christian life in light of the coming return of Christ. The Thessalonians were called to stand firm and live useful lives because the return of Christ might be in the distant future.

Circumstances of writing

Author

Paul stated to be the author of 2 Thessalonians (1:1). The greeting also mentions Silvanus and Timothy, but Paul was the primary author (3:17).

Background

See discussion under introduction to 1 Thessalonians. While there are few indicators about the date and place of writing of 2 Thessalonians, it was probably written from Corinth around AD 50–51, shortly after 1 Thessalonians. The mention of Paul, Silvanus, and Timothy together in the salutation, as was the case with 1 Thessalonians (1 Thess. 1:1), supports this conclusion. An additional support for this view is the mention of a previous letter, which was probably 1 Thessalonians (2 Thess. 2:15).

Message and purpose

Paul wrote in part to encourage the Thessalonian believers to stand firm for the truth in the midst of persecution and to assure them that God would judge those who were afflicting them (1:6–9; 2:13–15). Apparently, the Thessalonians thought they were already in the Day of the Lord (2:2). Paul assured them that they were not since certain end-time events had not yet taken place, and one was currently retaining "the lawless one" from appearing (2:6–7). This appears to be the primary impetus for the Letter. The fact that some people in the Thessalonian church had stopped working may suggest that their incorrect view was leading to lethargy and laziness (3:10–11).

The Letter is not long, and it does not give a definitive outline on the entire Christian faith. Paul wrote to meet a present need, and the arrangement of his Letter focused on local circumstances.

God's greatness. God loves people like the Thessalonians and has brought them into the church (1:4). He has elected them (2:13), called them (1:11, 2:14), and saved them. His purpose will continue to the end when they will be brought to their climax with the return of Christ and judgment. It is interesting to see so clearly expressed in this early Letter these great doctrines of election and call which meant so much to Paul. We also see his doctrine of justification behind the references to God counting the believers worthy (1:5, 11) and, of course, in his teaching on faith (1:3–4, 11; 2:13 ;3:2).

Salvation in Christ. Salvation in Christ is proclaimed in the Gospel and will be consummated when Christ comes again to overthrow all evil and bring rest and glory to his own. This great God loves his people, and he has given them comfort and hope—two important qualities for persecuted people (2:16). The apostle prayed that the heart of his converts would be directed to "God's love" (3:5), which may mean God's love for them or their love for God. Probably, it is God's love for them that was the primary thought, but Paul also noted a mutual love from the new believers. There are repeated references to the revelation (1:7; 2:6, 8). While the term is not used in quite the same way as in some other places, it reminds us that God has not left us to our own devices. It reveals what is necessary and has further revelations for the last days.

The second coming. The second coming is seen here in terms of the overthrow of all evil, especially the "man of lawlessness." Paul made it clear that Christ's coming will be majestic, that it will mean punishment for people who refuse to know God and who reject the Gospel, and that it will bring rest and glory to believers (1:7–10). In the end, God and righteousness, not Satan and evil, will be triumphant.

Paul made it clear that the Day of the Lord had not yet occurred. Several things must happen first—for example, "the apostasy" that occurs and the revelation of "the man of lawlessness" (2:3). Paul did not explain either. He was probably referring to what he had told the Thessalonians while he had been among them. Unfortunately, we do not know what he said then, so we are left to do some guessing. That a rebellion against the faith will precede the Lord's return is a well-known part of Christian teaching (Matt 24:10–14; 1 Tim. 4:1–3; 2 Tim. 3:1–9, 4:3–4).

Life and work. Paul had a good deal to say about people he called irresponsible and who appeared to be idle, not working at all (3:6–12). This may have been because they thought the Lord's coming was so close there was no point in working, or perhaps they were so "spiritual-minded" that they concentrated on higher things and let other people provide for their needs. Paul counseled everyone to work for their living (3:12). No doctrinal emphasis, not even that of Christ's return, should lead Christians away from work. People able to work should earn their daily bread. Believers are to work for their living and grow weary in doing good.

Contribution to the Bible

Second Thessalonians continues and further amplifies some of the same themes as 1 Thessalonians: persecution, sanctification, and end-time events associated with the second coming of Christ. One important difference is that 2 Thessalonians describes the "man of lawlessness" who will be revealed in the end of time and what restrains him from being revealed (2:1–12). The book also contains a lengthy discourse on the need for believers to have a proper work ethic to provide for their own needs (3:6–15).

Structure

The tone of Paul's Second Letter to the Thessalonians is markedly "cooler" than the first Letter. In the first Letter, Paul was enthusiastic about the Thessalonians' progress in the Gospel, and he offered calm advice about congregational life (1 Tim. 5:12–22). In this second Letter though, Paul expressed great concern about the spiritual state of the Thessalonian believers. He gave them a sharp rebuke about congregational life (2 Thess. 3:6–15). His style is typical of his other Letters—a doctrinal section followed by practical exhortation.

Outline

I. Introduction (1:1–12)
   A. Salutation (1:1–2)
   B. Thanksgiving (1:3–10)
   C. Intercession (1:11–12)
II. Instruction for the Thessalonians (2:1–17)
   A. Correction of a misconception (2:1–2)
   B. Revelation of the man of lawlessness (2:3–10)
   C. Judgment of unbelievers (2:11–12)
   D. Thanksgiving and prayer (2:13–17)
III. Injunction to the Thessalonians (3:1–16)
   A. Call to prayer (3:1–5)
   B. Warning against irresponsible behavior (3:6–15)
   C. Concluding prayer (3:16)
IV. Conclusion (3:17–18)

1 Timothy

Introduction

First Timothy, Second Timothy, and Titus have been referred as the Pastoral Epistles since the eighteenth century. It is reasonable to consider these Letters together since they have striking similarities in style, vocabulary, and setting. These Letters stand apart from other Pauline Letters in that they were the only ones written to Paul's Gospel coworkers. The Pastoral Epistles deal with church structure, issues and, unlike Paul's other Letters, were addressed to men serving in pastoral roles rather than to churches. But we must also recognize that these are separate Letters with their own distinctives. They were not written primarily to describe church structure or pastoral ministry (contrary to popular opinion) but to teach Christian living in response to the Gospel.

Circumstances of writing

Author

As stated in the opening of each Letter, these Letters were written by Paul (1 Tim. 1:1, 2 Tim. 1:1, Titus 1:1). However, many scholars today assume that Paul didn't write them. This opinion is based on the differences from his other Letters in vocabulary and style, alleged differences in theology, and uncertainties about where these Letters fit chronologically in the life of the apostle. But the differences in style and vocabulary are not troublesome when one considers that authors often use different vocabulary when addressing different groups and situations. Rather than addressing churches in these Letters, Paul was writing to coworkers who were in unique ministry settings. Even we would expect different vocabulary. Also, the traditional view of the historical situation in which Paul wrote these Letters is reasonable and defensible. Therefore, in spite of significant opposition by some scholars, there is a solid basis for accepting the Pastoral Epistle as Pauline.

Background

Paul most likely wrote these Letters after the time covered in the book of Acts. Acts closes with Paul in prison. Traditionally, it has been believed that Paul was released from this imprisonment, then continued his work around the Mediterranean, perhaps even reaching Spain (Rom. 15:22–29). During this time, he visited Crete and other places. First Timothy and Titus were written during this period of further mission work. Timothy had been left in Ephesus to handle some problems with false teaching there (1 Tim. 1:3–4). Titus had been left in Crete after the initial work to set up the church there (Titus 1:5). Eventually, Paul was imprisoned again, and this led to his execution. During this final imprisonment, Paul wrote 2 Timothy to request another visit from Timothy and to give final exhortations as he anticipated his martyrdom.

Message and purpose

In each of these Letters, Paul entrusted one of his younger workers in living out his faith and teaching others to do the same. Each Letter is concerned significantly with false teaching and its harmful effect in the church. In each Letter, Paul wrote to affirm his representative before the church to hold up the standard of right doctrine and to show that right doctrine must result in proper living.

In 1 Timothy, Paul directed Timothy to actively oppose false teaching. He also gave instruction on the type of behavior that should characterize those in church.

The Letter to Titus shows similar purpose, albeit briefer in scope. As Paul addressed the character of church members, he presented it in light of the work of Christ.

The message in 2 Timothy, Paul's final Letter, is quite different. It is much more personal, a letter from one friend to another. Paul was preparing Timothy to carry the work of ministry after he was gone. Several themes are found in these Letters:

The gospel. Paul expressed a concern for the truth of the Gospel. The term that Paul used in describing the Gospel in the Pastoral Epistles are not common in his other writings, but they are not unique to these Letters. He refers to the Gospel as "the Faith" (1 Tim. 3:9, 2 Tim. 4:7, Titus 1:13); "the truth" (1 Tim. 4:3, 2 Tim. 2:25, Titus 1:1); sound, healthy teaching (1 Tim. 1:10; 2 Tim. 1:13, 4:3; Titus 1:9, 2:1); godliness or sound religion (1 Tim 3:16, 6:3; Titus 1:1). Paul may have used these terms because they represent the phrases used by his opponents. As he used them, however, he renovated them for his purposes by attaching new meaning to them.

The Christian life. Paul emphasized the importance of a response of holiness to God's act of salvation (1 Tim. 2:15, 4:12, 5:10; 2 Tim. 1:9; Titus 2:12). Holiness calls for behavior that is both positive (Titus 3:8) and negative (2 Tim. 2:19) in emphasis.)

Church government. The church is presented as a united family ministering to its constituency and organized for service. The church is God's family (1 Tim. 3:5, 15), and believers are brothers and sisters (1 Tim. 4:6, 5:1–2, 6:2; 2 Tim. 4:21). Paul charged the church with responsibility to minister to the poor (1 Tim. 5:16) and to serve as a foundation of doctrinal ethical truth (1 Tim. 3:15). Leaders of the church are known as overseers or elders (1 Tim. 3:1–7, 5:17–19; Titus 1:5–9), and they are assisted by deacons (1 Tim. 3:8–13).

Contribution to the Bible

These Letters are rich theologically and ethically. One of their key contributions is the clear way they show the connection between doctrine and ethics, belief and behavior.

While these Letters were not intended to provide a detailed account of church government, they do provide some significant insights on this topic. The list of characteristics for overseers (1 Tim. 3:1–7, Titus 1:5–9) and deacons (1 Tim. 3:8–13) are the only such lists in the NT.

Structure

All three Letters follow the typical pattern of a Greek Epistle. While there are some lexical differences with many of Paul's other Letters, keep in mind that these Letters were written to specific individuals. One thing unique to the structure of these Letters is the focus on church leadership.

Outline of 1 Timothy

    I.   Greetings (1:1–2)
    II.   Introductory remarks (1:3–20)
        A.   Situation at Ephesus (1:3–17)
        B.   Charge to Timothy (1:18–20)
   III. Worship of the church (2:1–15)
        A.   Prayers (2:1–7)
        B.   Conduct of men and women (2:8–15)
   IV. Qualifications of church leaders (3:1–13)
        A.   Overseers (#:1-7)
        B.   Deacons (3:8–13)
    V.   The minister's job in tough times (3:14–4:16)
        A.   Stay focused on the Gospel (3:14–16)
        B.   Combat false teaching (4:1–5)
        C.   Set the example in service (4:6–16)
   VI. Duties toward others (5:1–6:2)
        A.   Relationships with various groups (5:1–2)
        B.   Responsibility toward widows (5:3–16)
        C.   Instructions for elders (5:17–25)
        D.   Instructions for slaves (6:1–2)

VII. Conclusion (6:3–21)
    A. Motives of false teachers (6:3–5)
    B. Warning against materialism (6:6–19)
    C. Final charge to Timothy (6:20–21)

2 Timothy

Introduction

See the introduction to the Pastoral Epistles before 1 Timothy.

Outline of 2 Timothy

I. Greetings and thanksgiving (1:1–7)
II. Not ashamed of the Gospel (1:8–12)
III. Loyal to the faith (1:13–18)
IV. Strong in grace (2:1–13)
V. An approved worker (2:14–26)
VI. Prepare for difficult times (3:1–9)
VII. The sacred Scriptures (3:10–17)
VIII. Fulfill your ministry (4:1–8)
IX. Final instructions (4:9–18)
X. Benediction (4:19–22)

Titus

Introduction

See the introduction to the Pastoral Epistles before 1 Timothy.

Outline of Titus

I.   Greeting (1:1–4)
II. Titus's ministry in Crete (1:5–16)
    A. Qualifications for elders (1:5–9)
    B. Warnings against the Judaizers (1:10–16)
III. Sound teaching (2:1–15)
    A. Moral responsibilities of believers (2:1–10)
    B. Salvation and Christian behavior (2:11–15)
IV. The importance of good works (3:1–11)
    A. Christian conduct in the world (3:1–7)
    B. Dealing with difficult people (3:8–11)
V.   Final instructions and conclusion (3:12–15)

Philemon

Introduction

This is Paul's only Letter of a private nature. It concerns a runaway slave, Onesimus, who had robbed his master, Philemon, and escaped from Colossae to Rome. There Onesimus met the imprisoned Apostle Paul. Paul wrote to Philemon concerning Onesimus. Paul sent both the Letter and Onesimus back to Colossae. By comparison to Paul's other Letters, Philemon is a little more than a postcard but comes from a tender heart of a friend writing as a friend rather than an apostle exercising his authority.

Circumstances of writing

Author

During Paul's two-year imprisonment in Rome (Acts 28:30), probably during AD 60–61, he wrote four prison Epistles, one of which was Philemon (the others were Colossians, Ephesians, and Philippians).

Background

References to Paul's being in prison at the time of writing are found in verses 1, 9–10, 13, and perhaps 23. Paul was kept under house arrest—what the Romans called free custody—in his own rented house as he waited for trial (Acts 28:30).

Although Paul addresses the Letter to Apphia, Archippus, and the church that meets in Philemon's house (vv. 1–2), the main addressee is Philemon himself, "for you" or "your" (vv. 2, 4–21, 23) is singular and refers to Philemon. Apparently, he was a prosperous businessman living in Colossae (Col. 4:9) whose household included several slaves and the household was large enough to accommodate meetings of the young church. He had been converted through Paul's ministry, perhaps by Paul himself (vv. 10, 19), and had become Paul's "dear friend and coworker" (v. 1) and "partner" (v. 17) in the Gospel service. Although the Letter is basically Paul's personal appeal to Philemon, the plural "you" (vv. 3, 22) and "your" (vv. 22, 25) indicate that the whole church would have listened to the reading and been witnesses of Philemon's response to Paul's requests.

Onesimus had apparently runaway and taken with him some of his master's money or possessions (vv. 15, 18). Perhaps attracted by the anonymity of a large distant city, he traveled to Rome seeking a life of freedom. His path crossed Paul's, and he became a Christian (vv. 10,16) and useful helper to Paul (v. 11).

An alternative view denies that Onesimus was a runaway looking for freedom. It instead suggests that he left Philemon and looked for Paul so that Paul could become his advocate regarding some serious loss Philemon had experienced. All along, Onesimus had intended to return to his master's household. Paul was, therefore, not guilty of harboring a fugitive slave. But on this view, we would expect Paul to reassure Philemon that Onesimus had always intended to return.

Message and purpose

This Letter has served as an inspiration for the liberation of slaves. Paul's clear preference was to keep Onesimus with him (v. 13), but he recognized that Philemon was his legal owner and decided to send him back (v. 12), so Philemon could either reinstate him as a slave who was now also a Christian brother (vv. 15–16) or else set him free for further service to Paul back in Rome (vv. 13, 20–21). Onesimus returned with this Letter to his master, knowing that Paul was confident of Philemon's "obedience" (v. 21) but also knowing that neither forgiveness nor reinstatement nor emancipation was guaranteed.

Contribution to the Bible

Although it is the shortest and the most personal of Paul's Letters, Philemon was included in the New Testament canon for several reasons.

First, it illustrates the breaking down of social and cultural barriers that occurred between Christians (see Gal. 3:28). Paul, a highly educated Roman citizen, takes up the cause of a poor runaway slave whose life was in danger because of his theft and flight (Philem. 18). Social and cultural barriers are eliminated in Christian fellowship.

Second, it reflects early Christian attitudes toward slavery. Although Paul accepts (but does not endorse) slavery as an existing social condition and as a legal fact (see v. 12), he emphasizes Onesimus's higher identity as a Christian brother and sets the master-slave relationship on a new footing (v. 16) and so, ultimately, undermines the institution of slavery. This contrasts with dominant views of the ancient world. For instance, Aristotle defined a slave as a "living tool, just as a tool is an inanimate slave" (*Nicomachean Ethics*, viii.11.6).

Third, it shows a skillful pastor at work. Paul gives up his apostolic right to issue commands (vv. 8–9) and prefers to appeal to Philemon's free choice (vv. 10, 14) to follow his Christian conscience in deciding how his love should be expressed (vv. 5, 7). He identifies with Onesimus, his spiritual son (v. 10), calling him a "part of myself" (v. 12) and guaranteeing to repay his debts (v. 18–19), and he gives his request to Philemon in the hearing of the whole local church (vv. 1–3, 22–25).

Fourth, it pictures the heart of the Gospel (v. 16–19). When we come to God in repentance and faith, he gives us a new status and welcomes us as if we were Christ. What we owe God, he had debited to Christ's account. Christ assumed personal responsibility for the full repayment of our debt to God.

Outline

Hebrews

Introduction

The Epistle to the Hebrews is a tribute to the incomparable Son of God and an encouragement to the author's persecuted fellow believers. The author feared that his Christian readers were wavering in their endurance. The writer had twofold approach: (1) He exalted Jesus Christ who is addressed as both "God" and "the Son of Man" and is thus the only one who can serve as mediator between God and man, and (2) he exhorted his fellow Christians, "let us go on the maturity" and live "by faith."

Circumstances of writing

Author

The text of Hebrews does not identify its author. What we do know is that the author was a second-generation Christian, for he said he received the confirmed message of Christ from "those who heard" Jesus himself (2:3). Because Paul claimed his Gospel was revealed directly by the Lord (1 Cor. 15:8, Gal. 1:12), it is doubtful that he was the author of Hebrews. The author was familiar with Timothy, but he referred to him as "our brother" (13:23) rather than as "my true son in the faith" as Paul did (1 Tim. 1:2).

Scholars have also proposed the following persons as author: Luke, Clement of Rome, Barnabas, Apollos, Timothy, Phillip, Peter, Silas, Jude, and Arstion. Ultimately, it does not matter that the identity of the author is lost. We should be satisfied with the fact that early Christians received the Letter as inspired authoritative scripture, and its value for Christian discipleship is unquestioned.

Background

The author of Hebrews knew his recipients well since he called them "brothers" (3:12, 7:5, 10:9, 13:22) and dear "friends" (6:9). Like the writer, they were converts who had heard the Gospel through the earliest followers of Christ (2:3). Scholars have speculated that those to whom the book was written were a breakaway group such as a house church that had separated from the main church. Another theory holds that the recipients were former Jewish priests who had converted to Christianity and that they were considering a return to Judaism (at least to conform to certain practices) in order to avoid persecution from fellow Jews. Another theory holds that the group was not necessarily Jewish since Gentile Christians also revered the OT as Scripture.

Regarding when the book was written, it is clear that the fall of Jerusalem (AD 70) had not yet occurred. The destruction of the temple would have been mentioned if it had already occurred for it would have strengthened the Letter's argument about Christ's sacrifice spelling the end of the temple sacrificial system. The public persecution mentioned in 10:32–34 implies one or two possibilities for dating the book. We know that the Roman emperors Nero and Domitian (in AD 64–68 and 81–82, respectively) persecuted Christians. Most likely, Hebrews was written during the persecution under Nero, perhaps just before the destruction of the temple.

Message and purpose

The author of Hebrews wanted to exalt Jesus Christ. A verbal indication of this desire is the consistent and repetitive usage of the Greek word *kreitton*, which means "more excellent" "superior" or "better." This word is the common thread that binds together the complex and subtle theological argumentation of the book. In comparison to everything else in the divine plan for creation and redemption, Jesus Christ is superior. The author described the superiority of the new covenant to the old covenant because he wanted his readers to remember that Jesus Christ is the fulfillment of the law and God's promises in the OT. In this light, readers should be careful about "recrucifying the son of God and hold Him to contempt" (6:6). The author wanted to move these believers from their arrested state of development into a pattern of growth in their relationship with Jesus Christ.

Contribution to the Bible

No other book in the NT ties together OT history and practices with the life of Jesus Christ as thoroughly as the book of Hebrews. Just as Jesus Christ taught that the OT was fulfilled in himself (Matt 5:17–18, Luke 24:27), so the author of Hebrews taught that the old covenant was brought to completion in the new covenant (7:20-*:13). Hebrews also shows that because the old covenant has been fulfilled in the new covenant, it is actually "better" (7:22). The new covenant was made superior by Jesus Christ's ministry.

Structure

In conclusion, in the book of Hebrews, the author wrote, "Brothers, I urge to receive this message of exhortation, for I have written to you briefly" (13:22). If the literary style of Hebrews indicates anything, it is that it is a written theological sermon. It is not so much a Letter—although it certainly ends like one—because it has no opening subscription as was the norm with ancient letters. Hebrews instead begins with an introductory essay about the superiority of Jesus Christ (1:1–4). However, its capacity to encounter the reader's soul indicates it is more than just a literary essay. Indeed, it has a definite sermonic character since it expounds the Scriptures at length in order to challenge the reader to faith and faithfulness. The sustained development of a complex, holistic theology of the covenant indicates that Hebrews is a written theological sermon that discloses the broad sweep of God's grand redemptive plan for humanity.

Outline

I.   The superiority of the Son of God (1:1–2:18)
   A.   The exaltation of Jesus Christ (1:1–4)
   B.   The divine nature of the Son (1:5–14)
   C.   The human nature of the Son (2:1–18)
II.   Superiority of the Son's faithfulness (3:1–4:16)
   A.   The faithfulness of the Son (3:1–6)
   B.   A warning (3:7–19)
   C.   The way forward (4:1–16)
III.   The superiority of the Son's work (5:1–6:20)
   A.   The work of the Son (5:1–10)
   B.   The call to maturity (5:11–6:3)
   C.   The way forward (6:4–20)
IV.   Superiority of the Son's priesthood (7:1–10:39)
   A.   The superiority of his order (7:1–19)
   B.   The superiority of his covenant (7:20–8:13)
   C.   The superiority of his ministry(9:1–28)
   D.   The superiority of his sacrifice (10:1–18)
   E.   The way forward (10:19–39)
V.   The superiority of the Christian faith (11:1–12:2)
   A.   The hall of heroes (11:1–40)
   B.   The way forward (12:1–2)
VI.   The superiority of the Father's way (12:3–29)
   A.   The work of God (12:3–13)
   B.   The way forward (12:14–29)
VII.   The superiority of the Christian life in church (13:1–25)
   A.   The way forward (13:1–19)
   B.   A blessing from the author (13:20–25)

James

---◦◦◦---

Introduction

The book of James is a wonderful companion piece to Jesus's teachings as recorded in the four Gospels. James has a strong ethical emphasis that is consistent with the moral teachings Jesus gave to his disciples. James also mirrors the sometimes harsh denunciations that Jesus spoke against religious hypocrisy. Like Jesus's teachings, the book of James is both a source of exhortation and comfort, reproof and encouragement. Finally, James is known for being extremely practical, yet it contains some of the most profound theological truths of the New Testament.

Circumstances of writing

Author

James is named as the author in 1:1. A number of NT personalities were named James, but only three are candidates for the authorship of this book. James the son of Zebedee died in AD 44, too early to have been the author. No tradition names James the son of Alphaeus (Mark 3:18) as the author. This leave James, Jesus's brother, also called James the Just (Mark 6:3; Acts 1:14, 12:17, 15:13, 21:18; 1 Cor. 15:7; Gal. 2:9, 12), as the most likely candidate.

This James is identified as Jesus's brother in Matthew 13:55, Mark 6:3, and Galatians 1:19. Though he was not Christ's follower during his early ministry (John 7:3–5), a post-resurrection appearance convinced James that Jesus is indeed the Christ (Acts 1:14, 1 Cor. 15:7). James later led the Jerusalem church (Gal. 2:9, 12), exercising great influence there (Acts 1:14, 12:17, 15:13, 21:18; 1 Cor. 15:7; Gal. 2:9, 12).

Background

James was probably written between AD 48 and 52, though nothing in the Epistle suggests a more precise date. James's death in AD 62 or 66 means the Epistle was written before this time. Similarities to Gospel traditions and Pauline themes are suggestive. If Mark was written around AD 65, and time is allowed for the events of Acts 15 and 21 to have occurred between Paul's first and second missionary journeys, a date between AD 48 and 52 seems most likely.

The reference to "the 12 tribes in the dispersion" (1:1) suggests the Letter was written to Jewish Christians living in or around Palestine. James led the Jerusalem church, so it is likely that the audience lived in that area (including Antioch). The reference to a synagogue in 2:2 also suggests that his audience were Jewish Christians. References to their circumstances (e.g., oppression by wealthy landowners [5:1–6]) could refer to congregations anywhere in the Roman Empire. However, Semitic word order, quotation from the Septuagint, and the overall dependence of the Epistle on the Jewish wisdom tradition suggests a specifically Jewish Christian audience.

Message and purpose

As a general Epistle, James was addressed to a broad audience (Jewish Christians) rather than a specific audience (e.g., Christians at Ephesus only). There is an obvious concern to address internal and external difficulties being faced by Jewish Christian congregations. Externally, they were facing trials (1:2), particularly oppression of various sorts exerted by wealthy landowners. It does not appear that the oppression was religious in nature. Internally, it appears that dissension was caused by lack of self-control (1:13–17), uncontrolled speech, and false teaching led to a misunderstanding of true religion

(1:19–27, 2:1–4, 3:1–8), favoritism toward the wealthy (2:1–13), and selfish ambition that led to murder and criticism (4:1–12).

Contribution to the Bible

James continually called for obedience to the law of God. He never referred to the ceremonial law but to the moral law. While some people think James is at odds with Paul about the Christian's relationship to the law, both authors actually combine to give us a solid understanding of the OT law. Paul showed believers that Christ met the demands of the law and, thus, brings us to salvation. James showed the believers that their obedience to God's moral standards is an indication of a living faith, which is a life lived in step with the one who met the demands of the law. Some choose to oversimplify the distinctions between OT and the NT and say the OT is grounded works, and the NT is grounded works of faith, but James brings both testaments together to show that faith and works are integrally related in both the old and the new covenants.

Structure

The book of James is a Letter (an Epistle), though the greeting conforms to the ancient Greek form exemplified in Paul's Letters, especially Galatians. The greeting identifies the author as James, including a title demonstrating the source of his authorship ("as a slave of God and the Lord Jesus Christ"), names the recipients ("the 12 tribes in the dispersion"), and conveys "Greetings" (1:1). Epistles were often used as means of spurring the recipients to change in behavior or belief based on the authoritative word and guidance of the sender. The book of James has been compared to OT wisdom literature. While there are wisdom elements in James, such as comparing the wisdom of the world with the wisdom that comes from God, it also contains exhortations and prophetic elements not common to wisdom literature.

Outline

I.   Salutation (1:1)

II. Surviving trials and temptation (1:2–18)
    A. Facing trials (1:2–12)
    B. God and temptation (1:13–15)
    C. Demonstrate God's good gifts (1:16–18)

III. Authentic religion (1:19–2:26)
    A. Show maturity of character (1:19–21)
    B. Put faith into action (1:22–27)
    C. Showing partiality and favoritism (2:1–13)
    D. Practice good works (2:14–26)

IV. The need for wise teachers (3:1–18)
    A. Teachers and control of the tongue (3:1–12)
    B. Teachers and wisdom from above (3:13–18)

V. Peace with God and one another (4:1–17)
    A. Pride and humility (4:1–12)
    B. Our will and God's will (4:13–17)

VI. Discipline in the Christian life (5:1–20)
    A. The hazards of wealth (5:1–6)
    B. Persevere under trial (5:7–11)
    C. Avoid swearing (5:12)
    D. Reach out to God in prayer (5:13–18)
    E. Minister to the wayward (5:19–20)

1 Peter

Introduction

First Peter is considered one of the General Epistles. This Epistle provided encouragement to suffering believers living in Northern Asia Minor who faced intense persecution. The Letter encourages faithfulness while under oppression. Specifically, God's holy people should lead distinctive lifestyles as temporary residents in a foreign land. Although they will suffer for Christ while in this non-Christian world, they should remember that heaven is their future homeland.

Circumstances of writing

Author

The author of 1 Peter identified himself as "Peter, an apostle of Jesus Christ" (1:1). He viewed himself as a divinely ordained, directly commissioned, authoritative representative of the Lord Jesus himself. Several statements in the Letter indicate that it is the Peter who played a prominent role in the Gospels who is the author. For example, he called himself an "elder and witness" to Christ's sufferings (5:1). Further, he described Christ's crucifixion with an intimate knowledge that only a disciple would have of that event (2:21–24).

Several expressions in 1 Peter reflect Peter's experiences with Jesus. For example, the exhortation for elders to shepherd God's flocks (5:2) evokes the charge that Jesus gave Peter in John 21:15–17. Moreover, the command to "clothe yourselves with humility" (5:5) may recall the episode in John 13:2–17 where Jesus washed the disciples' feet. Several themes in 1 Peter can also be found in Peter's sermon in the book of Acts. For example, God is the One who judges impartially (1:17; cp. Acts 10:34) and who raised him from the dead and gave him glory (1:21; cp. Acts 2:32–36). Christ is the stone that the builders rejected (2:8; cp. Acts 4:10–11).

Objections to the Letter's authorship by Peter are inconclusive and cannot be proven. The claim that someone wrote this Letter using the apostle's name as a pseudonym cannot be sustained. A number of early church leaders—e.g., Irenaeus, Tertullian, and Clement of Alexandria—accepted the Letter as authentic. Further, the early church soundly rejected the practice of writing under an apostolic pseudonym as forgery. In light of the above, the Epistle should be accepted as genuinely written by the Apostle Peter. Silvanus may have in some fashion helped Peter write the Letter while serving as his secretary (Greek, *amanuensis*), but more likely he was merely the letter carrier (5:12).

Background

The recipients of 1 Peter are identified in 1:1. Peter wrote to "the temporary residents dispersed in Pontus, Galatia, Cappadocia, Asia, and Bithynia." These were Roman provinces located in the northern part of what is now modern Turkey, unless Galatia includes the Galatia in the southern region of Asia Minor.

These people were likely persecuted Gentile Christians. They had earlier been involved in idolatry (4:3), were ignorant (1:14), and "empty" (1:18) before they came to Christ and formerly were not "a people" but now were God's people (2:9–10).

The reference in 1 Peter 5:13—"the church in Babylon, also chosen, sends you greetings"—suggests Rome as the place of the Letter's origin. "Babylon" was used cryptically to refer to a place of exile but specifically for Rome. Other possibilities for Babylon include the cities of Babylon in Mesopotamia and Egypt, but these places are highly unlikely because we have no record of Peter ever being in those places. First Peter was probably written sometime between AD 62 and 64. While Paul was under house arrest from AD 60–62, he did not refer to Peter in Rome. Peter likewise did not mention Paul being in Rome, only Silvanus and Mark were his companions (5:12–13). These facts suggest Peter wrote 1 Peter sometime after AD 62 and before the writing of 2 Peter.

The theme of suffering appears throughout 1 Peter. The recipients of the Letter are the sufferers in four of its five chapters. Given a composition date of about AD 62–64, 1 Peter was written during the persecution of Christians under Nero's reign. The persecution arose in Rome and was spreading into Asia Minor.

Message and purpose

Peter wrote to encourage suffering believers in Asia Minor to stand firm in Christ in the midst of persecution. He urged them to do so by focusing on their spiritual privileges and, more specifically, the place where their rights and privileges lay: the next life. Believers in Jesus are "temporary residents" (Greek, *parepideymoi* [1:1, 2:11]) and "strangers" (Greek, *parokoi* [2:11]), in this world, a land of sojourn where they have no real rights or privileges. Inheritance rights, privileges, and justice for Christians belong to another realm to which God has delivered believers—heaven, their ultimate home.

First Peter emphasizes that suffering is normal for believers because they are temporary residents in this world. As such, they lack and receive no justice in this foreign land. Though suffering occurs on earth for temporary residents, their inheritance and exaltation await them in their eternal homeland.

Contribution to the Bible

Peter's intent in writing was to strengthen believers in the midst of suffering and persecution they were facing. His message to them continue to speak to modern believers, reminding us of our heavenly hope and eternal inheritance in the midst of sufferings. We are called to holiness and a life of love. We are also called to glorify God in our daily lives and to imitate Christ.

Structure

The structure of 1 Peter has been a subject of discussion from the earliest history of the church. The diversity of outlines illustrates the task of exegesis is not merely science but also an art. Peter wrote this Letter with a typical opening for a letter (1:1–2) and then began the next major section (1:3–2:10) with a blessing (1:3). The two succeeding sections are marked by "dear friends" (Greek, *agapetoi* [2:11, 4:12]), and as noted earlier, the segment from 2:11–4:11 conclude with a doxology and "amen." The fourth section of the Letter also end with a doxology and "amen" (5:11) before the closing.

Outline

I.   Opening (1:1–2)
II. Called to salvation as exiles (1:3–2:10)
  A. Called for salvation (1:3–12)
  B. The future inheritance is incentive to holiness (1:13–21)
  C. Living as new people of God (1:22–2:10)
III. Living as strangers in a hostile world (2:11–4:11)
  A. The Christian life as a battle and witness (2:11–12)
  B. Testifying to the Gospel in the social order (2:13–3:12)
  C. Responding in a godly way to suffering (3:13–4:11)
IV. Persevering in suffering (4:12–5:11)
  A. Suffer joyfully in accord in God's will (4:12–19)
  B. Exhortations to elders and the community (5:11)
  C. Concluding words (5:12–14)

2 Peter

Introduction

Second Peter, one of the general Epistles, emphasizes practical Christian living. To this end, Peter wrote to warn against false teachers and the negative influence they can have on moral living. The Letter emphasizes true knowledge of God while facing false teaching and encourages readers to maintain Christian virtue in the midst of the world's vice.

Circumstances of writing

Author

The author of 2 Peter plainly identified himself as the Apostle Peter (1:1). He called himself "Simeon Peter," (1:1) a name not generally used of the apostle (elsewhere only in Acts 15:14). The spelling is Semitic and lends a sense of authenticity to Peter's Letter. Moreover, it was natural for Peter, as a Semite, to use the original form of his name. Peter designated himself as "a slave and apostle of Jesus Christ." He viewed himself as a servant submitted to Christ's lordship and as a divinely ordained, directly commissioned, authoritative representative of the Lord Jesus himself.

The Letter contains several personal allusions to Peter's life. He mentioned that his death was close (1:14), described himself as an eyewitness of the transfiguration of Jesus (1:16–18), quoted the words of the voice from heaven at this event (1:17), indicated that he had previously written to the Letter's recipients (whom he called "dear friend" in 3:1), and also called Paul "our dear brother" (3:15). This suggests that the author was close to Paul. Such references point to Peter as the author.

Many contemporary scholars, however, reject Peter as the author of this Letter. They argue, for example, that

1) the personal references to Peter's life are a literary device used by someone who wrote under the apostle's name in order to create the appearance of authenticity;
2) the style of Greek in 2 Peter is different from that of 1 Peter;
3) the reference to Paul's Letters as a collection (3:15–16) point to a date later than Peter's lifetime; and
4) 2 Peter was dependent upon Jude.

If this is true, Peter's authorship is problematic.

In response to these objections, one should consider that

1) the early church soundly rejected the practice of writing under an apostolic pseudonym, regarding it outright forgery;
2) Peter may have had help in writing 1 Peter (1 Pet. 5:12) and not in writing 2 Peter, which would lead to different styles in his Greek;
3) rather than the whole collection, Peter may have referred only to those Pauline Letters that were known at the time of writing; and
4) Jude may have borrowed from Peter, or both may have used a common source.

All of these evidences suggest that 2 Peter should be accepted as authentic.

Background

Unlike 1 Peter, 2 Peter does not mention specific recipients or refer to an exact destination. The apostle referred to his Epistle as the "second letter" he had written to his readers (3:1). If the letter written prior to 2 Peter is 1 Peter, then he wrote to the same recipients ("the temporary residents dispersed in Pontus, Galatia, Cappadocia, Asia, and Bithynia" [1 Pet. 1:1]). But if the previous letter is a reference to some other Epistle that is now unknown, we cannot determine with certainty to whom or to where 2 Peter was written.

Peter likely wrote 2 Peter from Rome, where church tradition placed the apostle in his later days. Because he mentioned that his death was near (1:14), it seems that the Letter was written just before his death. Tradition places the date of Peter's martyrdom at about AD 66 during Nero's reign (ruled AD 54–68).

Second Peter's literary relationship with Jude is debated. What one decides about this issue inevitably affects the authorship and date of each Letter. Both Epistles are strikingly similar in content. Thus, if 2 Peter borrowed from Jude and the later book was written somewhere between AD 65 and 80, the Apostle Peter could not have been the author of 2 Peter. The use of 2 Peter by Jude, however, possess no problem for authorship or dating. Jude may have borrowed from 2 Peter, or both authors may have used common source.

Peter wrote this Letter shortly before he died (1:14) and, though not mentioned, possibly while in prison. He wrote to the Christian friends confronted with the threat of false teachers who were denying Christ's saving work and second coming. As an eyewitness of Jesus's life (1:16–18), Peter sought to affirm for his readers the reality of Christ's return and to remind them of truths they might otherwise forget (3:1).

Message and purpose

Peter cautioned believers to beware of false teachers with their bogus doctrines and licentious lifestyles. The temptation to a sinful lifestyle so concerned Peter that shortly after his first Letter, he followed up with this one. Peter also warned against denials of Christ's return with its accompanying judgment. He urged his readers to make every effort to grow in the knowledge and practice of the Christian faith.

Contribution to the Bible

Peter made strong connections with the OT and challenged his audience to live authentic Christian lives. Peter had been with Jesus when Jesus first spoke of his return (Matt 24–25), and he gave emphasis of the surety of his second coming.

It is the word of God that holds the forefront of this short Letter. Peter does this in chapter 1 by emphasizing knowledge (vv. 3, 5, 6, 8, 12, 20–21) and its divine origin; in chapter 2 by showing its historicity (vv. 4–8); and in chapter 3 by indicating Paul's Letters are equal with "the rest of the Scriptures" (vv. 15–16). Peter insisted on the importance of the Scripture for guiding and preserving our faith.

Structure

Second Peter is a general Letter with typical features of salutation, main body, and farewell. What is missing is an expression of thanksgiving. Its style is that of a pastoral letter, driven by the needs of the recipients, rather than some type of formal treatise.

Outline

I.   Greeting (1:1–2)
II.   Building on faith with godly qualities (1:3–11)
III. The Apostle Peter's testimony (1:12–21)
IV.   Warning against false teachers (2:1–22)
V.   Certainty of Christ's return (3:1–10)
VI.   Christ's return impels us to holy living (3:11–18)

1 John

Introduction

John's first Letter addresses a setting in which some people in the local church had departed the fellowship (2:19), apparently because their doctrine, ethic, devotion, or some combination of these conflicted with those of the church. John wrote in part to stabilize the situation. He reaffirmed and enlarged on key theological truths, particularly the doctrine of Christ. He extolled love and emphasized the necessity for belief to be matched by action. A personal relationship with Christ is the foundation of the Christian's life, and out from this grows obedience to divine commands. True faith, proactive ethics, fervent love for God and people—most of the Epistle revolves around one or more of these three emphases as the author instructed, admonished, and encouraged his readers.

Circumstances of writing

Author

Ancient manuscripts are unanimous in naming John as the author of 1 John. This was understood to be John the son of Zebedee, "the beloved disciple" who was also the author of the fourth Gospel. The style and vocabulary of 1, 2, and 3 John are so close to that of John's Gospel that they beg to be understood as arising from the same person. Some contemporary scholars theorize that an "elder John" (see 2 John 1, 3 John 1), not the apostle, may have written these

Letters. Others speak of a Johannine school or circle as the origina-
tors of the Epistles of John (and perhaps Revelation too). But the
view of the best support is that Jesus's disciple John was the author.

Background

Second-century sources reported that around AD 70, the
Romans destroyed Jerusalem and the temple. John left Jerusalem
where he was a church leader and relocated to Ephesus. He continued his pastoral work in that region and lived until nearly AD 100.
Ephesus is probably the place John wrote the three NT Letters that
bear his name. They could have been composed at any time in the
last quarter of the first century.

Message and purpose

John made four purpose statements. First, he wrote to promote
his readers' fellowship and joy. "We are writing these things so that
our joy may be complete" (1:4).

Second, he wrote to help readers to avoid pitfalls of sin, yet find
forgiveness when they stumbled. "My little children, I am writing
you these things, so you may not sin" (2:1).

Third, he wrote to protect believers from false teachers. "I have
written these things to you about those who are trying to deceive
you" (2:26).

Finally, he wrote so they might know they had eternal life. "I
am writing these things to you who believe in the name of the Son
of God, so that may know that you have eternal life" (5:13). This last
purpose statement governs the other three and bring them together
in a unifying theme.

In summary, 1 John was written to confirm Christians in true
apostolic Christianity by helping them avoid the destructive beliefs
and behaviors to which some have fallen prey.

Contribution to the Bible

1 John maps out three main components of saving knowledge of God: (1) Faith in Jesus Christ, (2) obedient response to God's commands, and (3) love for God and others from the heart. This Epistle shows how Jesus expects his followers to honor him in practical church life and wherever God calls his people to go and serve.

Structure

It is widely believed that 1 John does not logically, methodically, or rigorously set forth and develop its arguments. For this reason, scholars are divided into the best way to structurally outline the Letter. It is the least letterlike of the three Johannine Epistles because of its lack of identification of the sender and the recipient. It is more likely unsystematic treatise. It often makes assertions along thematic lines, moves to related or contrasting themes, and then returns to the earlier topic or perhaps takes up a different subject altogether.

Outline

 I. The truth about Christ (1:1–4)
   A. An affirmation about the person of Christ (1:1)
   B. An affirmation about the author of the Letter (1:2–4)
 II. The believer's lifestyle (1:5–2:14)
   A. Fellowship with God (1:5–7)
   B. Confession of sin (1:8–10)
   C. Obeying the commands of Christ (2:1–6)
   D. Maintaining relationship with other believers (2:7–14)
 III. The believer's relationship to the world (2:15–27)
   A. Do not love the world (2:15–17)
   B. Beware of Antichrists (2:18–27)
 IV. Message for God's children (2:28–4:21)
   A. They will one day be like Christ (2:28–3:3)
   B. They are not to continue in sin (3:4–6)
   C. They must not be led astray by evil (3:7–10)

2 John

Introduction

The Second Epistle of John advises "the elect lady" (either a reference to a congregation or to a woman who own a house where the congregation met) to be fervent in Christian love (v. 5) and watchful of deceivers (vv. 7–8). The writer planned to visit the congregation soon (v. 12).

Circumstances of writing

Author

"The Elder" (v. 1) is the title the Apostle John applied himself late in life. (The Apostle Peter referred to himself the same way [1 Pet. 5:1]). No one other than the Apostle John was ever suggested by the early church as the writer of 1 John. Since there are so many similarities between 1 and 2 John, it is generally accepted that John also wrote the second Letter.

Background

Second John likely was written during the last two decades of the first century. During this era, John gave pastoral leadership to churches in the area of Ephesus. We have no way of precisely dating 2 John, but it is reasonable that it was written around the same time as 1 John or slightly afterward. Its tone reveals it to be a highly personal letter that reflects John's affection for these believers and his deep concern for their welfare.

Message and purpose

Like Jesus who wept over Jerusalem (Luke 19:41) and Paul who wrote "the daily pressure of his" care for all the churches (2 Cor. 11:28), John was concerned about this congregation. Would they neglect to embody God's love for one another? Would they fall prey to false teachers? Second John was apparently written to help readers follow through in their commitment to follow Christ.

John used six key words to tie together this Epistle. He repeatedly used the words *trust* (five times), *love* (four times), *commandment* (four times), *walk* (three times), *teaching* (three times), and *children* (three times). John's message is clear: he told his children to (1) walk in the truth, (2) obey God's commandments, (3) love one another, and (4) guard the teaching of Christ, and they would not be deceived by the Antichrist. John confirmed the spiritual safety of the believing community with a beginning and ending reference to their election by God (vv. 1, 13).

Contribution to the Bible

It is easy for a congregation to get off track. Second John reminds readers of the high priority of the most basic Christian outlook and activity—mutual love. Yet another priority is no less critical—the true Christian teaching. This Epistle strikes a short but strong blow for steadfastness, assuring that attentive readers would take the right steps to "receive a full reward" (v. 8).

Structure

Second John is an excellent example of hortatory or exhortation discourse which has the intent of moving readers to action. It follows the normal NT pattern for a Letter with an opening, main body, and closing. There are only two commands in this short Letter: a call to "watch yourselves" (v. 8) and the command "do not receive" those who plant false teaching (v. 10). There is a reminder to "love one another" in verse 5. This bears the force of an imperative, in part because of the close proximity of the word *command*, which occurs four times in verses 4–6.

Outline

    I.   Greeting and blessing (vv. 1–3)
    II.   Exhortation to Christian love (vv. 4–6)
    III. Warning about false teachers (vv. 7–11)
    IV. Impending visit and blessing (vv. 12–13)

3 John

Introduction

The shortest book in the New Testament, 3 John is a Letter with a kind but businesslike tone. "The Elder" sought to encourage Gaius, who was perhaps a pastor under his oversight. The Epistle gives mostly positive counsel but also warns against a power-hungry leader named Diotrephes. Truth, love, and God's goodness are prominent themes.

Circumstances of writing

Author

Same as the author of 1 and 2 John (see introduction there).

Background

Same as 2 John (see introduction there). The two short Epistles 2 and 3 John are often described as "twin Epistles," though they should be viewed as fraternal and not identical. There are some significant similarities worth noting. In both Epistles, the author described himself as "the Elder" (2 John 1, 3 John 1), and the recipients were those whom he loved "in truth" (2 John 1, 3 John 1). The recipients were a cause for great rejoicing by John (2 John 4, 3 John 3). They were "walking in the truth" (2 John 4, 3 John 3), and the Elder received good reports about them (2 John 4, 3 John 3, 5). Both Letters contain a warning (2 John 8, 3 John 9–11), and the Elder desired to see the recipients face-to-face (2 John 12, 3 John 14). Finally, both Letters convey greetings from others (2 John 13, 3 John 14).

Message and purpose

Third John is a personal Letter that revolves around three individuals: (1) Gaius, the recipient of the Letter; (2) Diotrephes, the one causing trouble; and (3) Demetrius, who was probably the bearer of the Letter. The purpose of the Letter was to give a word of exhortation to Gaius and encourage him not to imitate the bad example of Diotrephes. Instead, Gaius was to continue the good work he was doing in receiving and supporting the travelling teachers or missionaries.

Contribution to the Bible

This brief Letter of apostolic instruction underscores certain central Christian convictions: love, truth, faithfulness, the church, and witness. It also testifies to the God-centeredness of apostolic faith (vv. 7, 11). Jesus and the Spirit are not mentioned specifically (unless "the truth itself" in v. 12 refers to Jesus; see John 14:6, 1 John 5:20). But in the writer's view, Jesus and the Spirit were undoubtedly included in reference to God whose "truth" this Epistle appeals to so frequently (3 John 1, 3, 4, 8, 12).

Structure

The Letter follows the basic epistolary pattern with an instruction (vv. 1–4), body (vv. 5–12), and a conclusion (vv. 13–14). Though verses 1–4 clearly function as salutation, it is also possible to outline the Letter around the four personalities of the book. Verses 1–8 contain a multifold commendation of Gaius. Verses 9–10 condemn the high-handed and malicious autocracy of Diotrephes. Verses 11–12, taken as a unit, praise the godly Demetrius. Verses 13–14 close a glimpse into the heart of the Elder. Four men and their reputations (growing behavior) are the sum and substance of 3 John's subject matter. John constructed this Letter with the building blocks of key word repetition: "dear Friend" (vv. 1, 2, 5, 11); "truth" or "true" (vv. 1, 3, 4, 8, 12). Third John provides insight into a personal conflict that arose at the end of the first century and the strategy adopted by the Elder to resolve it.

Outline

    I.   Greeting to Gaius (vv. 1–2)
    II.   Joy at seeing Christians demonstrate the truth (vv. 3–4)
    III. Pressing issues (vv. 5–12)
         A.   Support for traveling ministers (vv. 5–8)
         B.   The problem of Diotrephes (vv. 9–10)
         C.   Commendation of Demetrius (vv. 11–12)
    IV. Impending visit and blessing (vv. 13–14)

Jude

Introduction

The Letter of Jude, one of the general Epistles, is very short. Until recently, scholars neglected it more than any other New Testament book. Jude sought to protect Christian truth and strongly opposed heretics who threaten the faith. The Letter's message is relevant to any age because believers should defend the Gospel vigorously. Jude bears an obvious similarity in content with 2 Peter, a book that also deals firmly with false teachers who were infiltrating the church.

Circumstances of writing

Author

Jude called himself "a slave of Jesus Christ" and a brother of James (v. 1). The James to whom Jude referred is not Zebedee's son. He can be ruled out of consideration because he was martyred at an early date (Acts 12:1–2). James to whom Jude refers is surely the well-known leader of the Jerusalem church (Acts 15:13–21, Gal. 2:9). This is significant for this James was Jesus's brother (Mark 6:3). If Jude was James's brother, then he was also Jesus's brother. Rather than call himself Jesus's brother outright, Jude chose humbly to designate himself as Christ's slave.

Background

Written to those who are "the called, loved by God the Father and kept by Jesus Christ" (v. 1). This designation is general enough to apply to Christian believers anywhere. But Jude clearly had a specific group in mind because he called them "dear friends" (vv. 3, 17, 20,) and addressed a situation that affected them. The readers were probably Jewish Christians because of Jude's several references to Hebrew history. Beyond this information, we don't know exactly who the recipients of the Letter were.

Jude is difficult to date precisely. If Jude, Jesus's brother, was the author, the Letter must be dated sometime within his lifetime. Any date for the Letter's writing must be also allowed time for the false teachings to have been developed. Jude may be dated reasonably somewhere between AD 65–80. Nothing in the Letter points a date of writing beyond this time. A date within Jude's lifetime rules out the viewpoint that the false teaching in question was second-century consticism.

Message and purpose

Jude had originally meant to write a letter on salvation to his friends. But he changed his plans when he learned of false teachers who had infiltrated the church (vv. 3–4). Because of their influence, he instead urged his readers to contend for the faith (3). Jude reminded his readers that they shared common salvation and alerted them to the need for vigilance in contending for faith. The reason the church must contend for the faith is that intruders were troubling the church. In verse 4, Jude introduced his readers to the opponents, pronounced judgment upon them, and outlined their vices. Verses 5–16 provide the evidence for what he said in verse 4. Three examples of God's judgment in the past are relayed in verses 5–7, and in verses 8–10, Jude stated that the opponents are compared to three men who went astray in the past: Cain, Balaam, and Korah. Verses 12–13 clarify that the character of the opponents place them in the same category as these infamous figures. Jude closed this section with the prophecy of Enoch which promises judgment on the ungodly (vv. 14–15). Jude correlated the lives of the adversaries with those who would experience Judgment (v. 16).

Contribution to the Bible

Jude is often overlooked because of its brevity. The book is also neglected because of unexpected features such as its quotation of Enoch and its allusion to the assumption of Moses. Some readers wonder how a canonical book could cite uninspired, nonbiblical writings. Furthermore, Jude's message is alien to many in today's world because Jude emphasized the Lord will judge the evil intruders who attempted to corrupt the church. The message of judgment strikes many people today as intolerant, involving, and contrary to the message of love proclaimed elsewhere in the NT.

Nevertheless, some of the Bible's most beautiful statements about God's sustaining grace are found in Jude (vv. 1, 24–25), and they shine with a greater brilliance when contrasting with the false teachers who had departed from the Christian's faith.

The message of judgment is especially relevant to people today. Jude's Letter reminds us that errant teaching and promiscuous living have dire consequences. Jude was written so believers would content for the faith that was transmitted to them (v. 3) and so they would not abandon God's love at a crucial time in the life of the church.

Jude's connection with 2 Peter is debated. What one decides about this issue inevitably affects one's beliefs about the authorship and dating of each Letter. They are strikingly similar in content. Thus, if 2 Peter used Jude, and the latter book was written somewhere between AD 65–80, the Apostle Peter could not have been the author of 2 Peter. But 2 Peter by Jude poses no such problem, allowing 2 Peter to fit within Peter's lifetime. It seems best to conclude that Jude borrowed from 2 Peter, or both used a common source.

Structure

The Epistle of Jude is a vigorous and pointed piece of writing. Scholars often remarked that its Greek is quite good, and Jude used that imagery effectively. The Letter bears a mark of a careful and disciplined structure and was directed to specific circumstances in the life of the church. Jude was steeped in the OT and Jewish tradition, and he regularly applied OT types and texts to the false teachers who had invaded the church (vv. 8, 12, 16).

Pseudepigraphal writings are noncanonical books not written by their purported authors. Jude cited from the pseudepigraphal book of 1 Enoch (1:9) in Jude 14–15. He likely also referred to an event found in the assumption of Moses (Jude 9). But this doesn't mean that Jude viewed these noncanonical books as authoritative scripture. Under the inspiration of the Holy Spirit, he simply used them as illustrations.

Outline

I.   Greeting and purpose (vv. 1–4)
II. Description of the false teachers (vv. 5–19)
III. Exhortation to faithfulness (vv. 20–23)
IV. Doxology (vv. 24–25)

Revelation

Introduction

The resurrected, glorified Son of Man (Jesus Christ) revealed himself to the Apostle John, who had been imprisoned "on the island called Patmos" (1:9). Christ's twofold purpose was (1) to "unveil a spiritual diagnosis for seven of the churches in Asia Minor with which John was familiar (chs. 2–3), and(2) to reveal to John a series of visions setting forth events and factors related to the end times (chs. 4–22).

Circumstances of writing

Author

The traditional view holds that the author of Revelation is the Apostle John, who wrote the fourth Gospel and the three Letters of John. Evidences for this view include

1) the writer referred to himself as "John" (1:4, 9; 22:8);
2) he had personal relationships with seven churches of Asia Minor (1:4, 11; chs. 2–3);
3) his circumstances at this time of writing (1:9) matched those of John the Apostle (who was placed in Asia Minor from about AD 70–100 by reliable historical sources from the second century AD); and

4) the saturation of the book with OT imagery and echoes implies a Jewish writer like John, operating overwhelmingly in gentile Asia Minor.

Background

The initial audience that received the book of Revelation was a group of seven local churches in Southern Asia Minor (1:11) (chs. 2–3). Some of these congregations were experiencing persecution (2:9–10, 13), probably under Roman Emperor Domitian (ruled AD 81–96). Others had doctrinal and practical problems (2:6, 13–15, 20–23). Also behind these surface problems was the backdrop of unseen but powerful spiritual warfare (2:10, 14, 24; 3:9).

Though some scholars have dated the book later, and a few have dated it earlier, commonly held dates of Revelation among evangelical scholars are the mid-'90s and the late '60s of the first century AD. The book's mid-'90s view is the stronger view, and it is held by majority opinion. Each view a different account of the persecution portrayed in the letters to the churches (2:9–10, 13). Substantial historical evidence shows that some of the churches were persecuted intensely by Nero in the late '60s. But the reference in 17:10 to seven kings, five of whom have fallen, support a date in the mid-'90s, during Domitian's reign.

While a case can be made for a late '60s date based on the Nero-related inferences and a possible reference to the Jerusalem temple in 11:1–2 (which may imply that the temple had not yet been destroyed, as it was by the Romans in AD 70), all other factors favor a date of about AD 95. Most notable among these factors is the tradition that John the Apostle was exiled to Patmos during a period of intensifying local persecution of Christians by the Emperor Domitian (ruled AD 81–96).

Message and purpose

Most of the book of Revelation focuses on events at the end of the age (eschatology) more than any other book in the Bible. But it also focuses on practical choices that believers and unbelievers must make in the course of their lives that have far-reaching consequences at the end.

Contribution to the Bible

The book of Revelation provides an almost complete overview of eschatology. There is much in this book about Christ, mankind and sin, the people of God (both the church and Israel), holy angels, Satan, and the demons. There is important material on God's power and tri-unity (i.e., Trinity), plus aspects of the work of the Holy Spirit and the nature of Scripture.

Structure

The book of Revelation previews its sequential structure in 1:19: "therefore write what you have seen, what is, and what will take place after this." From the Apostle's John vantage point in being commanded to "write," he had already seen the vision of the exalted Son of Man (ch. 1). Next, he was told to "write" letters to the seven churches, telling each the state of their spiritual health (chs. 2–/3). Lastly comes the body of the book (4:1–22:5) which covers all the events that would "take place after this."

Outline

I.   Introduction—"what you have seen" (1:1–20)
   A.   Prologue (1:1–3)
   B.   Salutation and doxology (1:4–8)
   C.   The Son of Man and the churches (1:9–20)
II. Letters to the churches of Asia—"What is" (2:1–3:22)
   A.   The church in Ephesus (2:1–7)
   B.   The church in Smyrna (2:8–11)
   C.   The church in Pergamum (2:12–17)
   D.   The church in Thyatira (2:18–29)
   E.   The church in Sardis (3:1–6)

F.   The church in Philadelphia (3:7–13)

G.   The church in Laodicea (3:14–22)

III.   Vision of the end times—"what will take place after this" (4:1–22:5)

A.   The heavenly throne room (4:1–5:14)

B.   The opening of the seven seals (6:1–8:1)

C.   The sounding of the seven trumpets (8:2–11:19)

D.   The signs before God's final wrath (12:1–14:20)

E.   The seven bowls of God's wrath (15:1–19:5)

F.   The reign of the King of kings (19:6–20:15)

G.   The new Jerusalem (21:1–22:5)

IV.   Conclusion (22:6–21)

A.   The command not to seal the scroll (22:6–13)

B.   Washing robes and the water of life (22:14–17)

C.   Warning about adding to the prophecy (22:18–19)

D.   Closing assurance and benediction (22:20–21)

About the Author

David Alouidor is God's servant, spreading His word in a way to reach people for Him. He is an immigrant from Haiti. God is good all the time. Before studying the Bible, ask Him for guidance. He will help you.

Thank you!

CPSIA information can be obtained
at www.ICGtesting.com
Printed in the USA
BVHW071651110123
655992BV00006B/174